D0873775

TABLE OF CONTENTS

ACKNOWLEDGEMENTS

Many thanks to Milt Baker for his time, efforts, and tenacity in helping craft words, adding polish, and simplifying our rough, and many times, complex recitations; these same thanks also go to Rich Gano. Our thanks also extend to other friends and colleagues, who, each in their own way, were instrumental in the final draft: Brian Sheehan- Fortress Marine Anchors, Steve Bedford- Super MAX Anchors, Paul Luke- Luke Anchors, Robert Taylor, P.E., Kevin Raymond, Jim Lenard, and Constance and Peter Snavley.

Thanks also to Samson Rope Company, Yale Cordage, New England Rope Company, Peerless/ACCO Industrial Group, Columbus McKinnon Corporation, The Crosby Group, Campbell/Apex Tool Group and Suncor Stainless Incorporated for providing information on some of the more technical aspects involved with the gear used in anchoring.

Last, and by no means the least—thanks to the folks on the Trawlers and Trawlering forum who put up with what seemed like endless interminable attempts at our constant refinement of details for this book.

PREFACE

**Sailors say, "fair winds and following seas",
and riggers, "big blocks and fair leads",
but for those who anchor, it's "long scopes and hefty gear".**

There is little doubt that, if queried, there would be agreement among boaters that the skill to anchor securely, in heavy winds or light, is an important skill to possess, and we wholeheartedly agree.

Our initiation into anchoring began years ago, immediately after we finished building our first cruising boat, a 36 foot, carvel-planked cutter. Within three weeks of our launch, we were faced with anchoring for our first hurricane. Since our boat was engineless, we knew that once our anchor was down, our ground tackle had to hold, no "ands, ifs, or buts" about it.

Fortunately, we had followed the advice of Frank Luke, of the Luke anchor fame, for sizing our storm anchor, one of his 3-piece, fisherman-style anchors which, we are convinced, kept us from dragging. But, it was with our rope rode and snubber that we became concerned.

Even though we had up-sized the rope from that suggested in the "chart", the size of rope that we were using still did not seem to be adequate. With the extreme stretch that we were observing, we could not help but worry about how easily that rope could chafe through. As it turned out, we were fortunate; even as novices we managed to not drag, nor did our rode part.

As we searched for better solutions, we quickly discovered that although there is an abundance of information on the mechanics of how to anchor, there is a dearth of information on how to appropriately size the gear for trouble-free anchoring, particularly when conditions will reach into gale and storm force levels. Over time, we happily discovered that the answers are there, albeit at times hidden or easily overlooked, occasionally disguised, or in hard-to-access material.

As these solutions were integrated into our thoughts, and our gear upgraded, we also discovered that most of the problems that are associated with anchoring, along with much of the anxiety, simply disappeared. Yes, anchoring still requires effort, often at times when we would rather be doing something less demanding, but on the other hand, the peace-of-mind that comes with knowing that the boat is securely anchored, regardless of the conditions, is, as that commercial says, "priceless".

And it is not just us; over the years, an innumerable number of folks, after we had provided to them the same guidance that appears in this book, report back that they, too, have experienced the same results–more secure anchoring, fewer problems, as well as less anxiety.

We also came to the realization that there are two caveats to anchoring which seem to be overlooked, or maybe they are just unknown. One is that recommendations given for anchoring are usually, if not always, minimum requirements... starting points, not stopping points. The other is, stray below any minimum recommendation and you will probably find that successful anchoring will prove elusive, and the further you stray, the more elusive this goal. So your goal, every time that you anchor, should be to meet or exceed minimum requirements.

The following chapters are not intended to be a complete treatise on anchoring; the basic principles of anchoring are covered in many of the books on anchoring, a few of which are listed in Appendix 9– Other

Suggested Readings.

Unfortunately, there are critical shortages, gaps, in the information presented in these books, and filling these gaps is the focus of this book, making it, we might dare to say, a necessary companion volume to the others.

This book also includes many helpful hints, tips, concepts, and suggestions, even a few techniques that some would consider "unconventional", which can be employed when anchoring. High tech or special purpose gear may be the best in certain circumstances, but generally, we favor the use of commonly available gear as much as possible, which usually results in gear that is less expensive, is more flexible and adaptable, and may be more readily found in chandleries with limited choices.

This knowledge of how to choose this commonly available gear may prove invaluable, especially if you are forced to shop where your preference for a specific piece of gear is not available, at least not in a timely fashion.

We also highly recommend techniques that, over the years, have proven to be reliable, even though some may be time consuming or labor intensive to implement.

Will conforming to the recommendations found in these chapters guarantee that you will not drag or break free? No, that is not possible; since there is always a human element involved in anchoring, no guarantee can be given. But, we are confident that by following these recommendations, any bad experiences you might have had will be minimized, if not avoided.

However, it is also important to understand that these ideas are not the only way of doing things, and if ever a situation arises where a better idea can work, do not hesitate to use it. On the other hand, we are hopeful that if you see any ideas in these chapters which are improvements over what you are now doing, you will adopt them as your own.

This is your book, add to it, make notes in the margins, highlight sentences, dog-ear pages, bookmark sections, and if it will help, color in the pictures... make this more than just a reference book, make it your workbook. Granted, you may not fully comprehend all of the details from these chapters until you have gained some experiences, but that is of little consequence as long as you believe in the importance of the old cliché, "better late than never". Since some of the subtleties or nuances of many of the passages might have escaped your attention, go back and reread this book, often, if necessary.

To assist those boaters who may not be familiar with some of the terms that are used throughout the book, a glossary has been included.

So let's get started; but first, do you have your mantra? Every mariner should have a mantra for anchoring and here's a good one to adopt–

"anchoring is not a speed sport, nor is it for the lazy"...

"anchoring is not a speed sport, nor is it for the lazy"...

"anchoring is not a speed sport, nor is it for the lazy"...

"anchoring is not a speed sport, nor is it for the lazy"...

INTRODUCTION

A category IV hurricane was forecast to hit the area where a couple lived aboard their 36 foot cutter. They knew that if they kept their boat in its slip, a slip where there was no protection from the high winds, waves, and storm surge that could be expected from a storm of this magnitude, then their boat would probably sustain extensive damage, but more likely end up sinking.

They considered hauling their boat at one of the local boatyards, or anchoring in one of the few protected anchorages, but instead, this couple chose to anchor away from other boats. Though the location that they chose had a firm sandy bottom, which would provide good holding for their anchors, its downside was fetch, over ten miles of it.

Fortunately, by the time the storm arrived, it had weakened to a Category III hurricane, but on the other hand, it more than made up for its weakening by stalling, remaining in the area long after most other hurricanes would have passed on. Wow, what a ride that must have been!

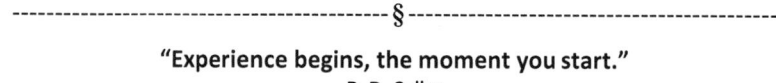

"Experience begins, the moment you start."
R. D. Culler

Granted, most of us are not likely to find ourselves anchoring in conditions like that mentioned above, but if you had to, could you?

What if less harsh, but more commonly occurring conditions, say a storm, a two day gale, or if one of those unexpected 45-knot squalls shows up unannounced while your boat is anchored, whether you are on it or are

1

ashore?

When reading about it, anchoring seems to be such a simple activity: stop the boat, lower the anchor, back off a short distance and set the anchor. Then, let out enough scope, attach a snubber, and secure the rode. Finally, to announce success, rig the anchor ball, or if night is coming on, hang an anchor light. Time consuming sometimes, but simple enough, right? Well, if this is the way it's done, why, so often, do boats drag? If you are thinking that there must be more to it, you would be right!

Successful anchoring requires more than just technique. Consideration must also be given to the strength and size of the myriad of components that will make up the ground tackle, in other words, not just the anchor, but also all of the other components necessary for its use. These components could include such items as rope, chain, bow rollers, chain stoppers, windlasses, cleats, maybe a Samson post or a pair of bitts. Then, too, don't forget about shackles, swivels, snubbers, anti-chafe materials, mousing wire, rode markers, buoys, trip lines, whipping thread, and maybe a splice or two.

Added to this list is the ability to calculate an adequate amount of scope, especially since the amount of scope with which one can get by with in light winds will be inadequate for heavier weather. Then, as if this isn't enough, in order to settle on which anchors to use, the mariner must give thought to the various factors that allow different types of anchors to be successful, or fail, in the various types of bottoms that might be encountered... jeez, the list seems endless.

So anchoring it isn't just an anchor; it's a complex, multipart system, wherein, not only must each component possess the strength to exceed Mother Nature's demands, but the components must also be able to interact with and rely on one another... a seemingly simple undertaking and one that can be eminently successful, but only if there is no flaw in the system.

At this point, we would like to introduce the concept of, what we call, *"The Big 5"*: It is around this concept of *"The Big 5"* that an adequate ground tackle system should be built:

- Anchor size
- Anchor design
- Strength of the components
- Scope
- Anti-chafe techniques

Each of *"The Big 5"* perform specific functions, functions that differ from one another and are not interchangeable. If you substitute one of these "Big 5" to perform the function of another you will usually increase, at times significantly, the odds that the anchor will drag or trip, or the boat will break loose.

In actuality, there is a "sixth" member of *"The Big 5"*– the use of multiple anchors. Although each of *"The Big 5"* must be considered every time an anchor is deployed, multiple anchors are involved only when the circumstances dictate their need.

If a boat breaks loose, or the anchor trips or drags, it is best to look first to *"The Big 5 + multiple anchors"*; chances are one or more of these will be at fault. Once the culprit(s) is identified, whether or not it is one of *"The Big 5 + multiple anchors"*, the necessary correction(s) can then be made, but only if the appropriate gear is onboard; and it should be.

This concept of *"The Big 5 + multiple anchors"* is an important concept, and worms its way through this book often going unstated. But, do not let this fool you, as these six factors should never be forgotten, nor ignored.

> ***This brings us to what we think is the most important***
> ***aspect of anchoring:***
> ***You must have the know-how to choose the gear that will***
> ***be more than adequate for the conditions.***

So, how do you go about choosing the right ground tackle? Some folks will just guess at the size of the gear that might be needed, and occasionally this method works. Others choose gear based on what they see on another boat. Success with this approach depends on several important factors, such as whether the boat is similar in size, whether the gear was successful for the other boat, and whether the conditions that will be encountered will be the same as those which the other boat had encountered.

Another option is to ask others for recommendations, but even if the person you ask is knowledgeable, does he or she really know enough to help you? Some crews with sufficient experience may be able to extrapolate from their own experiences, but since, as the wind's speed doubles, its force quadruples, this approach could be fraught with error. In fact, all of these ploys for choosing ground tackle are tenable at best, leaving, at times, potential for the gear chosen to be woefully inadequate.

Then, there are the charts or tables for sizing gear, based on the boat size. This sounds like the most promising approach, however, the chart may not provide, or the user may ignore, the "parameters" which were used to establish the size of anchor or other gear mentioned in the chart. In other words, without information on what wind speed, type of bottom, and the extent of protection from the seas, as well as a few other factors, on which these recommendations were based, the point at which this gear will become unreliable will be unknown. And, even if this information is provided, is there enough information to help you size all of the gear for conditions that exceed the parameters, other than possibly a nebulous statement such as "use a bigger anchor"?

So, if guessing is too inaccurate, mimicking may not work, the "expert" may not know enough, there is insufficient experience to fall back on, and the charts or tables may not be informative enough, what should you do? That is the focus of these chapters... to not only show you how to choose gear for ground tackle that will withstand just about any condition that your boat might encounter, but, what some might say is even more important, this information should also be applied to existing gear, to determine at what point it no longer should be relied upon.

Before we move on, we want to again stress that each element of *"The Big 5"*– size, design, strength, scope, anti-chafe techniques, and when appropriate, *multiple anchors*–plays a vital role in anchoring. As such, every time that the boat is being anchored, each should never be given less than full and due consideration.

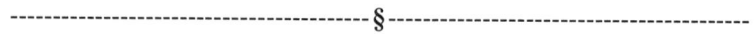

Regarding that boat mentioned at the beginning of this Introduction... was it a wise decision on this couple's part to reject all of those "safer" locations and instead anchor where they did? Well, some would say that it wasn't, but let's put the outcome of this crew's decision into perspective.

During this hurricane, this couple's boat did not drag or break loose, nor did any of its rodes or snubbers chafe, whereas, just about all of the boats that remained in the exposed marinas were severely damaged or destroyed. In the area's boatyards, many boats were damaged when they toppled over, or were toppled onto. In the more "protected" anchorage, that same anchorage that this couple had rejected, many of the boats that were anchored there broke loose or dragged, and of the few that did not, most were damaged by those that did.

Although this is an extreme example, it illustrates that even in extremely harsh conditions, anchoring can be done safely, though not necessarily comfortably. Also, if you think this was an isolated incident and that this couple was just lucky, please reconsider. At the time of the writing of this book these folks, who happen to be the same ones who authored these chapters, have anchored through five other hurricanes, countless other storms, gales, and squalls, not to mention having ridden out two other hurricanes while in a slip, all with the same good results that came from putting into practice the same ideas found in these chapters.

CHAPTER 1

THOUGHTS–ATTITUDES–TIMELINESS

A fellow who owned a thirty-eight foot sloop wanted to save some money, so, instead of continuing to pay slip rent, he opted to anchor his boat back in one of Florida's bayous. One night, when the wind was up, his boat dragged. Since he lived out of town, it was the local folks who were inconvenienced, chasing his boat down before any damage could be done, and then, after struggling to get it back to whence it came, re-anchoring it. Over the next year this happened again, twice more.

Eventually, months following these incidents, the owner reappeared on the scene and commenced to design a "better" anchor, one that was comprised of re-bar, chicken wire, and rocks. As you can guess, it didn't take long for this "anchor" to pull apart, allowing the boat to once again drag down the bayou, bouncing off docks, closely missing several other boats as it went. As in the previous episodes, it was the local folks who, once again, had to deal with this boat.

Months after this last episode, the owner finally showed up, only this time he commenced to solve the problem once and for all. After consultation with the manufacturer, he sunk the recommended helix anchor deep into the bottom and then attached his boat to it with pendants that are hefty enough to hold the boat even in the severe weather that this area can experience. Finally, a job well done… *kind of.*

---------------------------------------§--

"Always prepare sooner, not later."

Over the years, we have noticed that on the boats which do not drag or break free, the crews who man these boats seem to view anchoring differently than those crews on boats which do suffer these mishaps. Their choice of ground tackle always seems to be hefty, plentiful, has components that have the ability of being mixed and matched, and are replaced when worn, up-graded when necessary, and every piece is capable of exceeding that which Mother Nature will demand of it. These crews also seem to deploy their gear in a manner that is best for the circumstances, regardless of the effort required.

But, a strong argument can also be made that dragging, tripping or breaking free is not always the result of the wrong gear, sometimes it is simply the result of the wrong attitude... succumbing to those thoughts that are counter-productive to safe and secure anchoring.

> *This brings us to what we think is the second most important aspect*
> *of anchoring:*
> *You must have the motivation to acquire the appropriate gear, as*
> *well as the motivation to employ it prudently.*

One of the less-than-best attitudes that can get a boater in trouble is that of hoping *"maybe it won't happen",* and its cousin, which is even worse, *"maybe it won't happen... again".* As many boaters discover, often belatedly, is that it is better, every time, to instead think, *"what if it will happen",* and then act accordingly.

Then, there are those who claim *"it doesn't matter, the boat's insured".* This is the height of folly, since a boat that drags or breaks loose is a danger to other boats and property, as well as to the safety of any folks involved, whether they are on that boat or elsewhere. Then, too, is the consideration as to whether the insurance company will pay off, especially if the issue of negligence is involved, not to mention the lost boating time others may suffer because their boat was damaged. So, when the need to anchor presents itself, having the appropriate ground tackle and using it in a manner that is appropriate for the conditions is important, whether the boat is insured or not. This also goes for boats that are tied in a slip.

Another often heard statement, used to justify having dragged is that "the bottom had poor holding". Well, at least in our experiences and observations that label of "poor holding" is more often a result of a poor choice of gear, most likely the anchor; more about this in Chapter 7.

Ever hear *"In an emergency, anything is better than nothing"*, voiced to justify the use of inadequate ground tackle during squalls, gales, storms, and where they occur, hurricanes? Since the loads that these phenomena can put on ground tackle can be calculated, and gear is available to match these loads, there is no excuse for being inadequately prepared for any of these conditions. So, in our minds we cannot in good conscience label any of these natural phenomena as "emergencies".

Timeliness also plays an important role. For example, some of the gear required to prevent a boat of any size from dragging or breaking free is often of such size that few chandleries carry it in stock; therefore, it takes time to order the gear and get it in. In addition, whenever heavy weather is forecast, shelves often empty quickly of gear that is used for anchoring or for tying up boats. So the best way to get around these problems is not by putting off getting the necessary gear, but instead, to gather it early... months ahead of time. Then plan, organize and practice with it so that problems and deficiencies can be corrected prior to having to rely on it. In fact, getting this gear onboard before the boat is even launched is the prudent and smart thing to do.

In addition to acquiring the gear in a timely manner, putting it to use in a timely manner is also important. Everyone agrees that gear appropriate for any forecast heavy weather should be deployed expediently, but what many folks do not think about is that high winds can arrive without having been forecast, as in those quick-appearing squalls or one of those nighttime thunder(less) storms that often arrive unannounced. Though usually short-lived, such winds are often strong enough to overwhelm gear appropriate only for milder conditions, whether the boat is anchored or tied in a slip.

So, to avoid being ill-prepared, especially when the crew is ashore, asleep, or otherwise indisposed, be ready: regardless of the forecast, set ground tackle that will hold your boat, using gear that will hold with no need for intervention by the crew, regardless of the severity of the conditions that might develop. This is done by preemptively deploying a large-enough anchor, one that is appropriate for the bottom, using strong-enough gear and appropriate anti-chafe techniques, deploying enough scope, and if necessary, getting out more than one anchor. When tied in a slip, be sure that the lines are thick enough and that some manner for cushioning surge loads is used.

You'll see in the upcoming chapters, as long as you follow a few rules, sizing the gear for ground tackle is fairly straightforward. In addition, as you gain knowledge and experience, you will find that for any particular set of circumstances, there may not necessarily be only one way to anchor; in fact there may be several, any of which might be more than adequate, as long as nothing is done wrong.

And, a final thought: just about every sailor eventually learns that the answer to the age old question *"when should you reef"* is usually, *"when you first wonder if you should"*. Well, the same thought is also worthy of being applied to anchoring. To the question, *"when should the storm anchor be deployed"*, should also be answered with, *"when you first wonder if it should"*.

-------------------------------------- § ---------------------------------------

As to that boat mentioned at the beginning of this chapter, since the components used in ground tackle can age, chafe, or corrode to the point that any boat attached to it can break free, timely inspections of the gear is an important responsibility that the owner should not neglect. The problem now with this boat is that this gear isn't inspected by the owner, nor does he hire it done, at least not up to the time of the writing of this book.

The question remains as to whether this owner will eventually develop a better attitude toward anchoring and become more responsible. But, as of now, based on his past performance it does not look promising. If the local community is fortunate, maybe he will at least start displaying an anchor light.

CHAPTER 2

WORKING LOADS–PROOF LOADS–BREAK LOADS

Returning to a small cove on Florida's east coast after anchoring away from other boats for a hurricane, we noticed a fender floating where, prior to the storm, a 45 foot cutter had been anchored. Hauling in the float brought up a length of chain where, on one end, an anchor was attached, while at the other end, a twisted and broken shackle was barely hanging on.

When looking at this mangled shackle, there was little doubt in our minds that the owner of this cutter either had no knowledge of Working Loads, Proof Loads, and Break Loads, or no appreciation for the distinction between them. Otherwise, it is doubtful that he would have settled for a shackle whose sole requirement was not that it be strong enough, but rather that it be small enough to fit into one of the chain's links.

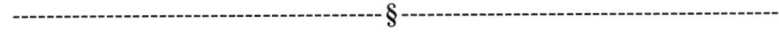

"Nothing too strong ever broke."
An old Maine Proverb

Strength is an integral consideration in the choosing of the gear for anchoring, and you should not make these decisions without being familiar with the following terms:

- Working Load Limit (WLL) - The maximum load for which an item is rated. Working Load Limit is also referred to as Work Load (WL), Safe Working Load Limit (SWL), Rated Capacity (RC), or

Rated Value (RV).

- Proof Load (PL) - The point at which an item, with a consistently increasing force, will start to deform.

- Break Load (BL) - The point at which an item, with a consistently increasing force, will break. Break Loads can indicate the rating for Ultimate Breaking Strength (UBS), Average Breaking Strength (ABS), or Minimum Breaking Strength (MBS).

- Safety Factor (SF) - The term "Safety Factor" often means different things to different people, but is best applied to indicate the difference between an item's Working Load Limit and its Proof Load. Having this distance between the Working Load Limit and the Proof Load provides for a little bit of strength kept in reserve– a margin of safety, so to speak–in case the Working Load Limit is inadvertently exceeded. *(Most components used in ground tackle, when new, will have a Safety Factor of 2, though for High Test chain, it is only 1.5.)*

- Design Factor (DF) - This term is accepted in the industry to mean the ratio between the Working Load Limit of an item and its Break Load, the point at which it will fail. *(Design Factors are typically 4:1, though some items have Design Factors as high as 5:1, and at least one at 6:1. High Test chain though is unique in that its Design Factor is lower, only 3:1.)*

> **Of these five terms, only the item's Working Load Limit (WLL) is used for sizing gear. This is done by choosing gear which has a Working Load Limit that equals or, better yet, exceeds the load that will be imposed on the ground tackle.**

If an item's Proof Load and Break Load are not to be used for sizing items, what purpose do these figures serve? For testing facilities, these

13

figures are used in calculations to determine if the item meets manufacturing standards. Otherwise, for us end-users, these figures serve no purpose and should be ignored.

The following paragraphs reveal several good reasons that, for sizing an item used in ground tackle, only its Working Load Limit should be used, in other words, why a healthy amount of strength needs to be kept in reserve:

- Bending Loads- Loads that are imposed on an item in a direction other than in a straight line relative to the item's axis. Bending loads are also referred to as side loads or bending moments. The need to consider bending loads is critical, as a bending load can cause an item to deform or break with as little as half of the load as that which would cause it to do so in straight-line pull.

- Shock Loads- A load that results from the rapid application of a force. Studies reveal that even mild shock loads can easily double or triple the load on the gear. Although these studies have been land-based, the implications of their findings provide for serious consideration when applied to ground tackle. For example, shock loads occur on ground tackle when, while the anchor is being set, a rapid application of engine power is applied, when seas, waves (surge loads), or wind gusts are present, or if the boat still has more than minimal way on, with the boat's sudden deceleration when the anchor sets.

- Resonance- When the boat's motion and the period of the waves closely correspond, then the boat's motion is in resonance with the wave. This resonance exacerbates the boat's motion, increasing the load on the ground tackle, at times significantly, even though the

14

size of the waves might remain quite small.

- Components in ground tackle undergo age, wear, and corrosion, some will suffer deformation, misuse, over-loading, intentional alteration, or other damage, any of which weaken these items.

- Mother Nature's Fickle Finger of Fate- Unlike in land-based use, where loads can be accurately calculated and tightly controlled, ground tackle is often subjected to loads that cannot reasonably be anticipated or accurately calculated. At times these loads occur singularly, while at other times there can be several unanticipated loads all imposed simultaneously upon the item. But in either situation, the result is that these additional loads, acting either singularly or in concert with one another, can be sufficient to overwhelm an item's Working Load Limit, even to the extent that the item may deform, even break.

Many of the items used in ground tackle have their Working Load Limits established by a manufacturing standard. However, there are a few items for which a Working Load Limit is seldom, if ever provided. The responsibility for establishing a safe Working Load Limit for these items falls on the user. The following items fall into this category:

- Rope- The American Boat and Yacht Council (ABYC) standards indicate that Nylon and polyester rope, used for anchoring, should be sized to have a minimum Design Factor of 8. In other words, rope should be chosen with a tensile strength that is at least 8 times that of the maximum load that will be on the ground tackle.

- For strong points and belaying points, such as cleats, bitts, Samson posts, bollards, and other like items, the ABYC recommends that their strength exceeds the highest load by a factor of at least two.

- The fasteners for strong points and belaying points should have a strength of at least 3 times that of the maximum load calculated for the ground tackle. For windlasses, their fasteners should also be 3 times that of the maximum rated load for the windlass.

- International Classification Societies recommend that an anchor's *holding power* should be twice that of the maximum load which will be on the anchor. However, for an anchor's *tensile strength,* choosing an anchor with a strength that is at least four times the maximum load that will be on the ground tackle is a wise thing to do.

- For all other items, where a Working Load Limit is not provided by the manufacturer, a good rule-of-thumb is to size the item so that its Work Load Limit will not exceed 25 percent of the maximum load that was calculated for that particular set of ground tackle.

A CAUTIONARY NOTE

Certain components are often intentionally subjected to bending loads. Because of this possibility, these components can be manufactured to have a Design Factor that is higher than is typical for most other components, as high as 6:1. However, this higher Design Factor is intended for use in land-based applications, where, as has been mentioned, the loads can be exactingly calculated, tightly controlled, and where unanticipated loads will be avoided. This is not the case with anchored boats, where the loads on the ground tackle are at best, a close estimation, and unanticipated loads often occur, especially during harsh weather. Therefore, no matter how high the number an item's Design Factor is, the item's Working Load Limit remains sacrosanct, and it is not to be exceeded when sizing the item for use in ground tackle.

CHAPTER 3

LOADS ON GROUND TACKLE

There we were, anchored on the banks in the Bahamas, out of sight of land, with miles and miles of fetch. Overnight, the wind had strengthened and clocked around. In the morning, after we got our anchor up and housed, we noticed that it was bent. Fortunately, in spite of having been bent, the anchor had not tripped.

When we had chosen this anchor, being the novices that we were, we had only considered its holding power. In hindsight, we actually had two problems. One was, regardless of its holding power, the fact that the anchor had bent was more than enough proof that it didn't have the strength that it needed; and the other problem was that we didn't have the faintest idea of how to determine what strength our anchors, nor for that matter, any other item in the ground tackle, needed.

Nowadays, things are different; determining the strength needed for our ground tackle is no longer a mystery for us and it doesn't have to be a mystery for you, either. Bent and broken ground tackle just does not have to be de rigueur in boating.

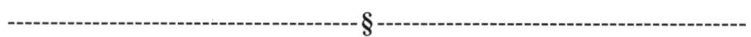

"When the wind and seas are getting up, bigger is better than smaller, stronger is better than weaker, longer is better than shorter, and doing it sooner is better than doing it later."

Determining the amount of strength needed for each component in the ground tackle, as well as the amount of holding power needed of the anchor, all begins with knowing the maximum load that will occur on the ground tackle.

Though engineers have a somewhat complicated formula for determining these loads, a simpler and just as acceptable method is to use one of the charts where these computations have already been worked out. Below, though in an abbreviated form, is one such chart:

LOADS ON GROUND TACKLE

Boat Size	Wind Speed (knots)	Load on Ground Tackle
20' sailboat	15	90 lb.
30' sailboat	15	175 lb.
40' sailboat	15	300 lb.
50' sailboat	15	400 lb.
20' sailboat	30	360 lb.
30' sailboat	30	700 lb.
40' sailboat	30	1200 lb.
50' sailboat	30	1600 lb.
20' sailboat	45	720 lb.

Boat Size	Wind Speed (knots)	Load on Ground Tackle
30' sailboat	45	1400 lb.
40' sailboat	45	2400 lb.
50' sailboat	45	3600 lb.
20' sailboat	60	1440 lb.
30' sailboat	60	2800 lb.
40' sailboat	60	4800 lb.
50' sailboat	60	6400 lb.

* *These figures are for a "traditional-sized" sailboat, anchored in sand, where there is moderate protection from seas and the boat having the freedom to oscillate.*

** *See Appendix 1 for other methods for calculating loads on ground tackle.*

WINDAGE

Since the data in the chart above is based on a "traditional-sized" sailboat, boats with more windage will have loads on their ground tackle higher than that reflected in this chart, as much as 50 percent higher. Boats that fit into this "higher windage" category are: trawlers, multi-hulls, houseboats, sail or power boats with greater beam than the "traditional-sized" sailboat, or sailboats with more than minimal freeboard or top-hamper from such things as pilot houses, wind generators, solar panels, enclosures, arches, or radar/TV/phone arrays. When this increased windage is present, if not already included, this additional load must be factored into the data when calculating the load on a boat's ground tackle.

PROTECTION FROM SEAS

Unfortunately, the terms used to indicate the "amount of protection from seas" that an anchorage can provide are nowhere near as precise as their importance suggests; nor can they be. On the other hand, these terms must convey enough understanding that the mariner can evaluate how much impact the anchorage's degree of protection will have on the boat, and thus the load on the ground tackle. The following terms, relative to the boat's size, are those that are in common usage, but the definitions are those of the author's:

- Poor protection- miles of, or unlimited fetch with no features that would block the wind or seas.

- Good protection- less than ¼ mile of fetch, with features that significantly reduce the wind or seas.

- Moderate protection- This term represents anchorages that would fall between those having "poor protection", and those having "good protection". In this category, a "sliding scale" must be used, ranking the anchorage based on the extent of protection offered, at best a subjective decision.

SURGE LOADS

When the boat is anchored where there is moderate protection from seas, it is generally accepted that approximately half of the load on the ground tackle will be caused by the wind; surge loads produce the other half of the load (*Oceanography and Seamanship,* Van Dorn). It should also be noted that, in *The Complete Book of Anchoring and Mooring,* Earl Hinz writes that multi-hull vessels will have a surge factor that is 15-20 percent higher than that mentioned above. Heavier displacement hulls will be affected to a greater degree than lighter displacement hulls, though there is no quantitative data that compares the difference between the two. For these boats, we are inclined to apply at least the same percentage as applies above to multi-hulls.

20

This information has a practical aspect. When a boat is "well" protected from seas, there may be as little as half of the load on the ground tackle as that noted in the load chart above. But, on the other hand, if the boat is anchored in a location where there is very little or no protection from seas, the loads will be higher, as much as 50 percent higher than that found in this chart. If necessary, the data that is being used should be adjusted by these percentages.

OSCILLATION

If a boat is secured in a manner that limits its freedom to swing into the wind, such as when anchored fore and aft, when the wind comes toward the beam, due to the increased windage, the ground tackle will have more load on it than that which is indicated by the chart above, as much as 50 percent more. When a situation like this will exist, this additional load needs to be included in the load calculations. It should be noted that this increase in the load on the boat applies to all motions that a boat can undergo, not just yaw. Boats made fast in a slip or alongside a pier are also impacted by this type of loading.

> *Once all of these factors have been considered, and the necessary data factored into the calculations, it is this load, the highest load calculated, that is the key to sizing every component in the ground tackle, from the anchor all of the way up to, and including, belaying points.*
> *This is done by choosing components which have WLLs that equal or exceed this highest load calculation.*

Up to this point, the loads on the ground tackle can be calculated with some degree of accuracy, albeit some along a sliding scale. But there are a few additional factors which are more difficult to quantify as to their impact on the ground tackle:

- Side loads- The loads derived from the calculations noted above are intended for use only when the load will be, relative to the center line of an item, in straight-line pull. As mentioned before, a side load, which we will also refer to as a bending load, can cause the item to bend or break with as little as half of the load as that required to do so in straight-line pull.

- Wind gusts- Typically, wind gusts can exceed the sustained wind speed by 30 percent, though some gusts will exceed sustained winds by 70 percent, even 100 percent. Since, as the wind's speed doubles, its force quadruples, ignoring the loads that wind gusts can place on the ground tackle can be a dangerous practice... maybe.

    The research relative to large vessel anchoring, as related by Robert Taylor, PE, a noted authority on large vessel anchoring, reveals that wind gusts, due to the need to overcome the resting inertia of a vessel, do not significantly increase the load on the anchor unless the gust persists for more than 30 seconds. With gusts that last less than 30 seconds, what little additional loading that occurs *on the anchor* should be easily handled if the anchor is sized as International Classification Societies suggest–that the anchor has twice the holding power than that of the maximum sustained load on the ground tackle.

    On the other hand, from our first hand experiences and observations, smaller boats, probably since they have much less resting inertia than that of their larger commercial or naval cousins, appear to be more easily affected by wind gusts, especially those gusts that reach into the upper strength levels. In addition, anchors, when used in a firm or hard bottom where they tend to bury relatively shallow, are more susceptible to being affected by wind gusts (and seas) than are those that bury deeper. Even if wind gusts do not significantly affect the anchor's holding, they more than likely affect the load on the rode, and as such, affect the rest of the components in the ground tackle, including belaying points.

- Duration- Winds of long duration allow the seas and waves to develop more fully than do winds that are of short duration. Because of their larger size, these seas and waves have more power; plus, the longer the wind blows, the more time Mother Nature has to wreak havoc on the gear. In conditions of long duration, the gear should be heftier than that which may otherwise be adequate for winds of the same speed, but of short duration.

- Currents- In *The Complete Book of Anchoring and Mooring*, Earl Hinz writes that the load on the ground tackle of a 40 foot boat in a five knot current amounts to about 300 lbs. For a 40 foot boat, using the data in the chart above, this load is the equivalent to being anchored in a 15 knot wind. Comparatively speaking, loads of this magnitude don't seem like much, but no matter how slight its drift, any current adds to the load on, and therefore impacts, the ground tackle, especially if any component is marginal in strength, or for the anchor, holding power.

But of greater concern with currents is the increase in windage created if the current yaws the boat more than 30-degrees. With this change in yaw, research reveals that the load on the boat

23

can increase by a factor of 2, but can go as high as 5 (Robert Taylor, PE).

In addition, a current that sets contrary to the wind can allow a rode to wrap on rudders, keels, props, pot warps, or other objects, dramatically changing the orientation of the pull on the anchor.

On the other hand, "wind-driven" currents contribute essentially little to the load on an anchored boat. As noted in *Bowditch*, a wind-driven current from a 60-knot wind where there is unlimited fetch is approximately 1.2 knots, a rather insignificant drag on the boat.

- Current vs Wind- Depending on the speed of these two forces, the seas created by each when they oppose one another, can be anything from small chop to large waves. Since these conditions add to the load on the ground tackle, they provide yet another reason to go "bigger" with the gear, rather than to accept using gear that may prove to be marginal, or worse, inadequate.

- Unanticipated Loads- As mentioned in Chapter 2, unlike in land-based use, where the loads can usually be exactingly calculated and tightly controlled, ground tackle is often subjected to loads that cannot reasonably be anticipated or accurately calculated. At times, these unanticipated loads occur singularly, while at other times there can be more than one, all imposed on the ground tackle simultaneously. In either case, whether occurring singularly or in concert with one another, these loads can reach magnitudes that may overwhelm a component's Work Load Limit, even its Proof Load, maybe its breaking point.

UP-SIZING COMPONENTS

Sizing items as we've so far outlined in this chapter may result in adjacent items that do not fit together. When this situation occurs, one remedy is to up-size the smaller item until it fits the larger item. Yes, the up-sized item will have more strength than what the calculations suggest is needed, but more strength is not a problem, whereas accepting an item that fits, although does not have adequate strength can be a big problem.

Other remedies for getting adjacent items sized such that they can mate together, are to: make adaptations to one of the items in order that the two will fit together (e.g., install oversized links in High Test chain); use smaller, but higher-strength connecting pieces (e.g., use high-strength [alloy] shackles in place of the more commonly available regular-strength [carbon] shackles); or, possibly join the items together using an intervening length of rope, sized appropriately for strength, and spliced to each.

ON BEING CONSERVATIVE

How conservative one should be when computing the load on the ground tackle is a personal decision. At one end of the spectrum would be day sailing in a small, limited area, only in pleasant conditions, and where well-protected anchorages or ready access to a mooring or a slip are plentiful. At the other end of this spectrum is a boat which spends nights at anchor in widely differing locations, wherein the anchorages are quite varied in protection, high winds may occur, and many, if not all, of these additional load factors may be encountered.

Fortunately, there is one rule that reigns supreme–those who "oversize" their gear seldom have the problems which often plague those who don't. But, first stop and think about the term "oversized" for a moment–if the gear does not bend or break or if the anchor did not drag, is the gear really "oversized"? Since the term "oversized" often imparts a negative connotation, maybe we should, instead, start using the term "big enough".

So, the loads on ground tackle, even for modestly sized boats, can be huge. When loads like this are anticipated, it is no wonder that the use of big, hefty gear comes highly recommended. If the boat can be located so as to not receive the full force of the wind or surge, so much the better, though it is important that you should not rely that this can always be arranged.

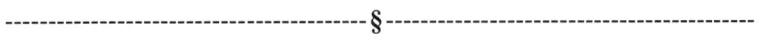

Have you been wondering why that anchor, mentioned at the beginning of this chapter, bent? This anchor had dug in so deep that it could not come around sufficiently to stay "in-line" as the boat changed direction, thus had a side load imposed on it. This anchor had a tensile strength that was more than adequate in straight-line pull, but as we discovered, it did not have the strength that it needed when the boat veered and a side load developed on the anchor; thus, it bent.

Since bent anchors are not reliable anchors, we immediately switched to using a different anchor. Eventually we were able to return that anchor into service, but only after it was straightened back to its original shape... however, this anecdote does not end here.

For years, we had been seeing reference to the idiosyncrasy for items to bend or break with less force when side-loaded than what it takes for them to bend or break in straight-line pull. Thus, about a year later, we had an epiphany while perusing a tensile strength chart provided by the manufacturer for this, as well as their other sizes of anchors. We noticed that the anchor one size up had more than twice the tensile strength than did the anchor that we had been using.

It was at this point that it dawned on us that this idiosyncrasy of things to bend or break with a lesser load when side-loaded can easily be overcome simply by up-sizing that piece of gear. Once the implications of this simple solution sank in, we replaced the now known-to-be-too-weak main bower with another anchor, one of the same design, only bigger, one strong enough to resist the side loads that our boat can impose on the anchor in 60-knot winds.

EXAMPLES - CHAPTER 3

In this, and where applicable, in other chapters, examples relevant to the chapter's topic will be presented. All of the examples will be based on a hypothetical 35 foot sailboat, modest in windage, anchored where it has moderate protection from seas and with the freedom to oscillate.

In this example, the load on this hypothetical 35 foot sailboat's ground tackle is calculated for four wind speeds:

- 15-knot winds- 225 lb. load on ground tackle
- 30-knot winds- 900 lb. load on ground tackle
- 45-knot winds- 1800 lb. load on ground tackle
- 60-knot, short duration winds- 3800 lb. load on ground tackle
- 60-knot, long duration winds- a component's Work Load Limit should be at least one size up from that required for 60-knot, short duration winds. If the component is already significantly over-strength for 60-knot, short duration winds, no increase in strength is required.

MODIFYING THE ABOVE EXAMPLES

- These figures for the loads on this hypothetical boat's ground tackle can be decreased by half if the "protection" from seas will be "good", but why bother!
- These figures for the loads on this hypothetical boat's ground tackle should be increased 50 percent if the boat has more windage than does a "traditional-sized" sailboat, if the boat will be anchored fore and aft, or if the protection from seas will be poor or absent.
- The figures for this boat's loads on its ground tackle represent the minimum Work Load Limit for every component in the ground

tackle.

- Rope, per ABYC standards, should have a tensile strength of 8x the load on the ground tackle. Anchors should have twice the holding power, but a tensile strength of four times that of the maximum load on the ground tackle. Belaying points should be sized to have twice the strength of that of the maximum load on the ground tackle, while the fasteners which secure any belaying points should have thrice the strength of that of the maximum load on the ground tackle. For the windlass, its fasteners should be three times that of the windlass' rated load carrying capacity.

- Should any of the figures for the load on this boat's ground tackle be at a component's upper end of its Work Load Limit, that component should be up-sized, at least one size up.

- If any component will be subjected to a side load, that component's WLL should be increased, at least one size up.

CHAPTER 4

CHAIN

Some years ago, as we finished building our first cruising boat, a 36 foot cutter, we made a decision to use all chain on its main bower. So we called up a local supplier, ordered some chain, and when it came in, got it stowed away. Little did we know just how lucky we had been; in our ignorance, we happened to have picked chain that worked well in our windlass.

After cruising for several years, we stopped to design and build another cruising boat, a 34 foot, sail-assisted trawler. Having installed the same type of windlass with the same size wildcat on this boat, as we had on the sailboat, we were able to transfer some of the chain from the sailboat to our new trawler.

Then, early in our shake-down cruise, we decided that we wanted to add more chain to our inventory. Specifying the same size chain that we currently had, we ordered additional chain from a chandlery. Much to our dismay, when we received this new chain it was different than what we had been using; it was the same "size", but matched neither our existing chain, nor our wildcat.

Because of this incident, our interest was piqued. As we delved into this subject, we realized how confusing the choice of chain can be for those who are, like we were, uninformed. It seemed that there was something mystical about choosing the right chain, but as we began to better understand this subject, we discovered how easy it can be to make the right choice.

-------------------------------------- § --

"Chain is only as strong as its weakest link."
Unknown

FIRST OFF, IS CHAIN REALLY NECESSARY:

- Chain costs more than rope, is heavier than rope and is not as easy on the boat's finish or the hands as is rope.

- Helping to get the anchor set is one reason that is often given for using chain; but getting the anchor set with an all rope rode can also be done, usually just by using a different length of rode when setting the anchor.

- In mild conditions, the catenary of a chain rode—the sag that comes from the weight of the rode—helps an anchor hold. But, the catenary of a rope rode can be improved by adding weight in the form of a kellet (see Appendix 5).

- Chain can be useful in limiting a boat's swing room, but with a rope rode, installing a kellet (see Appendix 5), deploying multiple anchors (see Appendix 7), or using a hammerlock moor (see Appendix 7) can also accomplish the same result.

- Many boaters think that a wildcat can be used only with chain, but there are wildcats that can function with either chain or rope. Even a windlass with a chain-only wildcat can often retrieve rope, if the rope is sized right.

- In the chain locker, the ability of chain to readily collapse on itself can be an advantage, but 8-plait (brait) or 12-braid rope also has this ability.

- If chafe is a concern, a larger diameter rope could be employed,

31

since large diameter rope is more chafe resistant than is smaller diameter rope, or a rope made from more chafe resistance material could be used.

SO WHY USE CHAIN AT ALL?

Chain is useful because it does have a couple of advantages over rope. When stowed, it takes up less room than rope, and chain is not as susceptible to chafe as is rope. If a windlass must be used and the wildcat cannot function with rope, then there is no other choice but to use chain in the windlass.

HOW MUCH CHAIN IS NEEDED?

If that portion of the rode which lies immediately adjacent to the anchor requires protection from chafe, only a few feet of chain need be installed at that end. For those who have a windlass and want to save weight or cost, or possibly the windlass is slow, so it is faster to bring the rode in by hand, it is often useful to have an all rope rode, except at the outboard end where, when the rode is "up and down", the length of chain need not be much longer than that necessary to reach the windlass; the remainder of the rode can be rope.

At the inboard end of the rode where it may chafe on a bobstay, hawse hole, chock, or anchor roller, or where it might be at risk of getting run over by a prop, then this end of the rode could benefit from having chain. But if chafe or damage is a concern along the entire length of the rode, or weight, cost, or speed of retrieval is not an issue, then it is probably best to use chain for the entire rode.

> **TIP:** If chain is needed, and more than one anchor will be deployed, each rode may require its own length of chain.

CHAIN'S LIMITING AFFECT ON ANCHOR DEPTH

Due to friction, a chain can limit the depth to which an anchor will bury, therefore reducing the anchor's holding power. This may not be much of a problem when you are anchoring in sand or other firm or hard bottoms, but as the bottom softens, where the anchor must bury deeper to develop its maximum holding power, this can become an issue.

Replacing a chain with wire cable, one with an appropriate Working Load Limit, the wire, creating less friction, will allow the anchor to bury deeper. If chain is to be used, and the anchor is to develop as much bury as possible, the chain should be sized no larger than its required Work Load Limit, and unless chafe is a concern, according to Robert Taylor, P.E.– acknowledged in a previous chapter–no more than ten feet of chain should be used, the remainder being wire cable or fiber rope.

ISO vs NACM CHAIN

Throughout the world there are at least 11 different standards to which chain can be manufactured, and when it is manufactured to any one of these standards there is assurance that the chain's dimensions and its strength are as specified. However, chain made to any one of these standards is not a guarantee that it will work in any particular wildcat or will mate with chain or connectors which are manufactured to another standard.

Although any manufacturer is free to make chain to any of these standards, the two standards which are commonly used to manufacture chain in the USA are the ISO standard and the NACM standard. *(ISO–International Standards Organization; NACM–National Association of Chain Manufacturers)*

The ISO standard is used to make chain which is often called ACCO chain, anchor chain, marine chain, or windlass chain, while the NACM standard is used to make chain that is often called industrial chain, generic chain, general purpose chain, and although it is a misnomer, transportation chain.

33

While ISO chain is generally found in chandleries or at marine suppliers, and NACM chain is usually found in hardware stores, home improvement centers, and industrial supply facilities, this is not a hard and fast rule, and you may find just the opposite. What can confuse the issue even more is that some sellers, just because the chain is galvanized, will call it "anchor" chain or even "windlass" chain, with no regard for its pedigree. And worse yet, some chain may be made to no recognized standard, then galvanized and sold as anchor chain, with its choice risky, since its dimensions, strength, or quality could be inadequate.

> **SCHEDULE 40 IS NO LONGER**
> In the past, High Test chain had been divided into two schedules, both having the same strength-Schedule 40 designation was used for NACM chain, while Schedule 43 designation was used for ISO chain. In 2005, a change was made, making the "schedule" designation for High Test chain the same for both NACM chain and ISO chain, to that of "Schedule 43". Even though the designation of "Schedule 40" has been dropped, this term still finds its way into common usage.

Though the difference in size between ISO and NACM chain seems insignificant, it can be critical when a windlass is involved. It is sometimes possible to mate the longer and narrower link NACM chain to a wildcat, but most recreational-boat wildcats are designed to fit the shorter and wider link ISO chain. So chances for a successful match between chain and a wildcat is more likely with ISO chain.

Another advantage that ISO chain has over NACM chain, as well as many imported chains, is that ISO chain, depending on the manufacturer, has thicker galvanizing–double-dipped–than does its NACM or imported cousins, thus its galvanizing will have a longer service life.

If, on the other hand, no windlass is involved, the link's dimensions then do not matter, so you can use either ISO or NACM chain, an option that can be attractive since NACM chain is not only more readily available, it is usually less expensive than ISO chain.

So, when you are searching for chain, regardless of where you shop it, it is important to ascertain to which standard the chain was manufactured–ISO, NACM, or to some other standard. If you can't determine this distinction by looking at a label on the chain's shipping crate, call the manufacturer and ask. If there is any doubt, and the chain's dimensions or its strength is important, look elsewhere for the chain.

If you are looking for chain outside of the USA, become familiar with the standards that apply in that country and how those standards will affect the chain's compatibility with any existing or future chain, connectors, and windlasses.

STRENGTH-TO-WEIGHT

As far as strength goes, there are essentially only two choices– low strength-to-weight chain, Grade 30, which is also called Proof Coil, G3, or schedule 30 chain; or higher strength-to-weight chain, Grade 43, which is also called High Test, G4, or schedule 43 chain. Both of these choices are available as either ISO chain or NACM chain.

ISO chain also includes an additional choice that NACM chain does not have–BBB chain, often referred to as Triple B. BBB chain has the same strength as does Proof Coil chain, they are both Grade 30, but the difference is in the links, which are shorter in BBB chain.

There are also higher strength-to-weight grades of chain– Grade 70, which is also called transport or binding chain, and Grades 80, 100, and 120. However, these higher strength-to-weight chains are available only as NACM chain, and with the exception of Grade 70, they have one big disadvantage–they become embrittled when galvanized, losing strength, and they will break with a lower load than that for which they are rated. To offset this loss of strength in Grades 80, 100, and 120, the chain has to be up-sized to regain the strength that will be lost when galvanized, thus also regaining most of the weight that might have been saved by using one of these higher strength-to-weight grades. Due to this quirk, it makes little sense to use Grade 80, 100, or 120 chain in ground tackle unless to fulfill a specific purpose other than weight savings.

As far as strength goes, it doesn't matter whether it is ISO or NACM chain, as chain of the same size and Grade will have the same strength. As an example, 5/16 Grade 30 chain, made to ISO standards will have a Working Load Limit of 1900 lbs., as will 5/16 Grade 30 chain made to NACM standards. As another example, 5/16 Grade 43 chain, made to either the ISO or NACM standard, will have a Working Load Limit of 3900 lbs.

There are other considerations which may help you make the choice between Grade 30 and Grade 43 chain. For Proof Coil (or BBB) chain to have

> **HIGH TEST vs HIGH TENSILE**
> Confusion often exists between the terms "High Test" and "High Tensile". The metal used to make G4 chain, as compared to G3 chain, has more carbon added to the iron, and once formed, the chain is then heat treated. Through both of these processes, G4 chain ends up having more strength than G3 chain. Being stronger than G3, it can be tested to higher strengths, thus the term "High Test" chain. On the other hand, "tensile" is essentially strength; G3 chain, being the lowest strength is "low tensile" chain, G7 chain, having the higher strength is "high tensile" chain, and G4 chain, having strength that falls in the middle is "medium tensile" chain. So, to avoid sounding like a landlubber, just remember that High Test and High Tensile are not the same!

the same strength as High Test chain, the Proof Coil (or BBB) chain would have to be up-sized, and this increase in size generally results in chain that is heavier and more expensive than High Test chain of the same strength.

On the other hand, using the larger size Proof Coil (or BBB) chain adds weight, an advantage over High Test chain of similar strength, as the additional weight will function as a "built-in" kellet. However, although this weight can be useful in milder conditions, this advantage is lost once the wind speed rises sufficiently (see Appendix 5). Then, too, if bringing in the rode by hand is a consideration, you should size the chain no stronger, thus no bigger than what the calculations require, and use G4 chain for its weight savings.

STAINLESS STEEL CHAIN

NACM standards also provide specifications for stainless steel chain, and if made to these standards, the chain's strength will be greater than Proof Coil chain (or BBB chain), but less than that of High Test chain. Since the 300 series stainless steel is specified in this standard, 316L stainless steel, if the chain will be used for an anchor rode, is the better choice.

This standard, in addition to providing the guidelines for strength, also provides the guidelines for dimensions, dimensions that are not compatible with most wildcats. But some companies, in addition to chain with those dimensions specified by this NACM standard, also manufacture stainless steel chain that is compatible with many windlasses by duplicating the dimensions of ISO Proof Coil, ISO BBB, and ISO High Test chain. However, even though the chain may match the dimensions of ISO High Test chain, it is still stainless steel and remains less strong than its High Test carbon steel chain cousin.

As long as the manufacturing standards for strength and quality assurance are followed, stainless steel chain in these duplicate sizes is an advantage for those who wish to use it as an anchor rode... *maybe.*

Stainless steel chain is a classic example of the adage–*just because you can, doesn't mean you should*! One weakness of stainless steel chain is that, especially in saltwater, it can develop small, essentially invisible cracks, especially around the welds. These cracks often result in "unexpected"

37

failure of the chain. Also, stainless steel chain, unlike carbon steel chain which has relatively good elongation qualities before it finally breaks, has very poor elongation qualities, which, once its Proof Load is exceeded, there is little stretch, providing poor warning that the chain had approached its failure point.

Another problem with stainless steel chain is that it can suffer from oxygen starvation, a situation that is encountered in water that has little movement, is polluted, or when the chain buries in the bottom. Without enough oxygen, stainless steel develops pitting and crevice corrosion, making the metal susceptible to failure, again, often without warning. Although 316 stainless steel is less susceptible to this problem than is 304, it can occur with either grade.

Thus, stainless steel chain is a questionable choice for use as anchor chain, particularly for frequent or long-term anchoring, or for use in permanent moorings.

MOORING CHAIN

Mooring chain, often referred to as "long link" chain, is a galvanized carbon steel chain, and it, too, is stronger than Grade 30, but less so than Grade 43. It is also usually more thickly galvanized than either NACM or ISO chain. An advantage to using mooring chain is that its links are wide enough and long enough to allow equal-strength, commonly available (carbon) shackles to be installed, not just in the end links, but anywhere along the chain.

However, there are no worldwide-accepted standards to which mooring chain is manufactured. As such, the strength and dimensions of mooring chain may vary from one manufacturer to another, although this is of no consequence as long as the chain and the shackles that fit it have the requisite Work Load Limit.

While it may be possible to use mooring chain as an anchor rode, trying to do so has several challenges:

- It comes only in a handful of sizes;
- It's hard to match to a wildcat because its links are larger than those in either Grade 30 or Grade 43 chain;
- Not all suppliers carry Mooring chain;
- It's more expensive than ISO and NACM chain.

HALLMARKS

Chain, as well as some connectors, manufactured to an industry standard will be marked with letters or numbers in order that the chain's strength and manufacturer can be identified. This is done by embossing the side of every "x" number of links with a *raised*

HALLMARK

COURTESY PEERLESS CHAIN COMPANY

identifying symbol, called a hallmark. Chain or connectors not manufactured to a standard will probably be marked with *indented letters or numbers* or not have a hallmark at all.

CHOOSING A CHAIN

Up to this point, picking a suitable chain is straightforward. If a windlass is involved, ISO chain has greater odds of fitting the wildcat; if no windlass is involved, then either ISO chain or NACM chain can be used, maybe even mooring chain.

If high strength-to-weight chain is desired, Grade 43 can be chosen, maybe even Grade 70. However, if weight doesn't matter but the ease of fitting shackles does, then pick Grade 30, or if a windlass isn't involved, maybe mooring chain can be used. But, hold on... what is meant by "the ease of fitting shackles"?

SHACKLES

Regular-strength, galvanized (carbon) shackles, the shackles that are most commonly found on shelves, if manufactured to an industry standard, are sized to fit and to equal in strength Grade 30 chain, be it ISO chain or NACM chain. But this is not so with Grade 43 (High Test) chain.

With High Test chain, no matter to which standard it is manufactured, the link's internal dimensions will not be significantly larger in size over the same size Grade 30 chain, but it will be stronger, so to match this increased strength, shackles must also be stronger, thus bigger. But the pins in these larger shackles are also bigger, so they will not fit High Test chain of comparable strength. Shackles which do fit, by necessity, are smaller, and thus have less strength than does the High Test chain to which they are fitted... boy, what a conundrum, and one that has resulted in the loss of many boats!

Of all of the methods available to mate equal-strength shackles with Grade 43 (or Grade 70) chain, the simplest is to either have oversized links installed in the chain (see Chapter 10) or to use high-strength (alloy) shackles (see Chapter 10). If the arrangement would work, it would be best to do both, since then, either type of shackle, regular-strength (carbon) or high-strength (alloy) can be used, in case one is difficult to obtain.

OTHER CONNECTORS

There may be times when you will need for sections of chain to be joined together. Except for mooring chain or chain with oversized links in its ends, this usually cannot be done using a single shackle; instead, two shackles, interlocked together, will most often be needed. For a more thorough discussion of connectors, including shackles, oversized links, and using rope as a connector, see Chapter 10.

SIZE

You have now come to probably the most important decision in choosing chain–what size to get? Make no mistake about it, it is not convenience, cost, space, weight limitations or any other contrived consideration that should be used to determine the appropriate size of chain that should be used... it is Mother Nature.

> *Once the maximum load that can be imposed on the*
> *ground tackle has been calculated (see Chapter 3), the chain's size*
> *can be chosen by finding a size of chain which has a Work Load*
> *Limit (WLL) that equals or exceeds this calculated load.*
> ---------------------------------------§---------------------------------------
> **See Tables 1-4 for a listing of ISO, NACM, Stainless Steel and Mooring chain's*
> *WLLs, dimensions, and strengths.*

WINDLASSES and WILDCATS

The use of a wildcat (gypsy) is limited to the size of chain it was designed to accommodate. So, to avoid the risk of being forced to use chain with a Work Load Limit less than the calculations suggest, it is best to first specify what size chain is needed, and only then locate a wildcat that will fit the chain.

Though it is possible to find wildcats that work with some sizes of NACM chain, it is often a "trial and error" process, and there is a chance that, when a fit is made, the chain's size and the wildcat's "stamped" size may not match. However, a mismatch like this is of no consequence if the combination works. As an example of a mismatched wildcat and chain, on our main bower, we have 5/16 NACM High Test chain, and though it is not a perfect fit, it works well in our horizontal windlass which has a wildcat that is stamped for 3/8 chain.

When purchasing a windlass, to be assured that a wildcat is available and will work with the size of chain required, a call to the windlass' manufacturer should first be made. It may even be necessary to send the windlass manufacturer a 2-3 foot sample of the chain so that it can be trial-fit by the manufacturer for assurance that their wildcat will work with the chain.

If the windlass is already in-hand, look for the stamp found on many wildcats indicating the size of chain it is designed for. On some windlasses, this stamping is located such that the wildcat must be removed to locate it, on others, it may be absent.

If there are no indications as to the size of chain required for the wildcat, the code is unrecognizable, or it is not clear as to whether ISO, NACM, or some other chain is to be used, the wildcat will need to have various sizes of chain trial-fit until the correct size is identified.

> **TIP:** By measuring the wire diameter of the link, as well as the inside length and inside width of the link, each to the hundredths of an inch, then comparing these dimensions to the manufacturer's standard, you can determine if the chain has exceeded its Proof Load. Once any link has exceeded its Proof Load, the chain is no longer reliable and needs to be replaced.

One way to do this is to remove the wildcat from the windlass and take it to a chandlery or chain supplier, where various sizes of chain can be trial-fitted. Or, order 2-3 foot samples of various sizes of chain from a supplier, even if there is an associated cost, and trail-fit them yourself. If this cannot be accomplished locally, send the wildcat, preferably insured, to a chain supplier for trial-fitting. Either is a less expensive way to go than just guessing and taking a chance on buying a significant amount of chain that will not be usable.

ROPE/CHAIN WILDCATS

For use in a rope/chain wildcat, the rope's diameter, if of 3-strand or 8-plait construction, will usually need to be twice that of the size of the chain. For example, 5/16 inch chain will probably require 5/8 inch rope spliced to it. If the rope is of 12-braid construction, due to its "hollow" center, which compresses when the wildcat's jaws grip the rope, this construction will usually need to be one or two sizes larger than that of 3-strand or 8-plait rope.

> **CHAIN RODE and NO WINDLASS**
>
> If you are using a chain rode and have no windlass, or maybe it's broken, but you do have access to a winch, consider using a messenger line as an alternative to a windlass. The messenger line is hitched to the rode, then lead to the winch. When the messenger line has been winched in as far as practical, the rode is temporarily stopped-off, and the messenger line is released from the rode, brought forward, re-attached to the rode, and the stopping cast off. Repeat this activity until the rode is brought in as far as you wish. A capstan, warping drum, tackle, or even plain old muscle power can be substituted for the winch. With this procedure, if time is of the essence, instead, buoy, then slip the rode for retrieval at a later time; otherwise enjoy this slow process of weighing anchor.

Under these guidelines, and using the ABYC's recommendation that the rope should have a Design Factor of 8, the rope's Working Load Limit will most likely be less than that of the chain. When this is the case, the rope then dictates the maximum load to which the ground tackle should be subjected. If a rope with a higher Working Load Limit is required, a larger rope will need to be spliced in, but you must understand that this size rope may not work in the wildcat that was sized for the chain. This issue, more than likely, will necessitate the rode's deployment and retrieval by hand, though the assistance of a warping drum, winch, or tackle might be sought.

BENDING LOADS

Chain, even when sized correctly, has the same vulnerability as does

43

every other component in the ground tackle–vulnerability to bending loads. Since a chain's strength is rated only for straight-line pull, any load that is not in-line with the long axis of any of its links will result in a bending load on the link. This bending load can cause the link to deform or break with less force than that for which it is rated.

Bending loads can occur if a link gets caught on the edge of a chock, hawse hole, over the framework of an anchor roller, or as sometimes happens, when caught on a rock, piece of coral, or maybe even an engine block lying on the bottom. A kink in the chain also creates a situation in which a bending load will be forced on the involved links; therefore it is critical to avoid loading a chain in which kinked links are present.

If bending loads cannot be avoided, then the chain's Work Load Limit, thus its size, must be increased in order to counter the weakness that is caused by the link(s) being loaded off-axis. How much? Go up at least one size and possibly more, that is, if keeping the boat from breaking loose is the goal.

STRETCH

The matter of stretch needs to be addressed, as protecting the windlass, ground tackle, and belaying points from the forces produced by surge loads and wind gusts is the providence of stretch. For any rode with too little stretch, chain included, stretch is easily provided by the installation of a long, stretchy, snubber. This snubber can be made of 3- strand, 8-plait, or 12-braid Nylon line (see Chapter 5).

ATTACH IT TO THE BOAT

The bitter end of chain rode can be attached to the boat by shackling, bolting, or lashing it directly to a fitting in the rode locker or, maybe elsewhere. This is not the best method because it does not provide for the quickest or the most convenient way of releasing the rode.

A better alternative is to attach a rope pendant to the bitter end of the chain and then secure the other end of this pendant to the boat. This arrangement allows for the rope to be more easily untied or cut, freeing the chain.

This pendant arrangement can be even more advantageous if the length of the pendant is long enough to reach up on deck, as then a trip below to free the rode can often be avoided. And, if this length of rope is "long", say around 30 feet in length, it will cushion the shock when the boat fetches up hard should the rode undergo an uncontrolled run out. If this pendant is attached using a round turn or two, followed by a rolling hitch, the pendant can usually be released even when under a load. These ideas apply also to rope rodes.

SAFETY-SAFETY-SAFETY

Picture your hand, sans a few fingers because one or more got caught between the chain and the wildcat; then remember this picture every time that windlass work is required. To avoid an injury such as this, grip the chain only with finger tips (Stevedore grip). This Stevedore

STEVEDORE GRIP

grip is not just applicable for working around windlasses, it can be of benefit anywhere that a finger can get caught between the rode and something harder than the finger, and is useful when working with rope, too. This grip may not always be possible, but whenever it is, it minimizes the chances of sustaining a finger-ruining injury.

By planning for the worst, getting gear that will live up to what

Mother Nature will demand of it, then using it prudently, not only will make life safer while you're anchored, but it will also provide you with more peace-of-mind.

EXAMPLES - CHAPTER 4

In this, and where applicable, in other chapters, examples relevant to the chapter's topic will be presented. All of the examples are based on a hypothetical 35 foot sailboat, modest in windage, anchored where it has moderate protection from seas, and with the freedom to oscillate.

In the following examples, various sizes of chain are listed for our hypothetical sailboat's ground tackle. These sizes of chain are based on just a few of the wind speeds which were used for load calculations in Chapter 3: 45-knot winds, 60-knot, short duration winds, and 60-knot, long duration winds. Data for the following examples of chain are from Tables 1, 2, and 4 which are located at the back of this book.

45-KNOT SUSTAINED WINDS-
Minimum Work Load Limit required for each piece of gear is 1800 lbs.

- ISO Proof Coil (G3) chain-   5/16 inch chain (1900 lb. WLL)
- ISO BBB (G3) chain-   5/16 inch chain (1900 lb. WLL)
- ISO High Test (G4) chain-   1/4 inch chain (2600 lb. WLL)
- ISO G7 chain-   not available
- NACM Proof Coil (G3) chain-   5/16 inch chain (1900 lb. WLL)
- NACM BBB (G3) chain-   not available
- NACM High Test (G4) chain-   1/4 inch chain (2600 lb. WLL)
- NACM G7 chain-   1/4 inch chain (3150 lb. WLL)
- Mooring (long link) chain-   3/8 inch chain (3700 lb. WLL)

60-KNOT, SHORT DURATION WINDS-
Minimum Work Load Limit required for each piece of gear is 3600 lbs.*

- ISO Proof Coil (G3) chain-   1/2 inch chain (4500 lb. WLL)
- ISO BBB (G3) chain-   1/2 inch chain (4500 lb. WLL)
- ISO High Test (G4) chain-   5/16 inch chain (3900 lb. WLL)

- ISO G7 chain-   not available
- NACM Proof Coil (G3) chain-   7/16 inch chain (3700 lb. WLL)
- NACM BBB (G3) chain-   not available
- NACM High Test (G4) chain-   5/16 inch chain (3900 lb. WLL)
- NACM G7 chain-   5/16 inch chain (4700 lb. WLL)
- Mooring (long link) chain-   3/8 inch chain (3700 lb. WLL)

It is our thinking that, with the inclusion of the Safety Factor that is present in the Load Table, plus that of the item, choosing a component with a Work Load Limit that is "very slightly" less than the load found in any of these tables will not, at least in any appreciable manner, increase the risk of the item failing.

60-KNOT, LONG DURATION WINDS- Minimum Work Load Limit one size up from that required for 60-knot, short duration winds; if the component is already significantly oversized for those wind speeds, no increase in size is required. *

- ISO Proof Coil (G3) chain-   1/2 inch chain (4500 lb. WLL)
- ISO BBB (G3) chain-   1/2 inch chain (4500 lb. WLL)
- ISO High Test (G4) chain-   3/8 inch chain (5400 lb. WLL)
- ISO G7 chain-   not available
- NACM Proof Coil (G3) chain-   1/2 inch chain (4500 lb. WLL)
- NACM BBB (G3) chain-   not available
- NACM High Test (G4) chain-   3/8 inch chain (5400 lb. WLL)
- NACM G7 chain-   5/16 inch chain (4700 lb. WLL)
- Mooring (long link) chain-   1/2 inch chain (6000 lb. WLL)

It is our thinking that, with the inclusion of the Safety Factor that is present in the Load Table, plus that of the item, choosing a component with a Work Load Limit that is "very slightly" less than the load found in any of these tables will not, at least in any appreciable manner, increase the risk of the item failing.

48

CHAPTER 5

ROPE– RODES-SNUBBERS-FLOAT-TRIP LINES

As we returned from anchoring for a storm, we motored past an area where, before the storm, a 36 foot sloop had been anchored, but now this sloop was no longer there. Looking several miles across the water to the opposite shore, we spotted this same sloop, beached, ten feet away from the now back-to-normal water level. When we went over to see if we could help, one of the first things that we noticed was a few feet of the anchor rode lying limp over the bow, the end thoroughly frayed and raveled.

"Rode chafed through", the boat's owner informed us. As we inspected the frayed ends of the rope, we also noticed shiny areas on the surface of the rope, as well as hard little nodules on the ends of some of the frayed fibers, both indicating that the rope had gotten hot enough to melt. When we asked why he had chosen that particular size of rope, he said, "I used the size indicated on the chart".

Yes, indeed, he had used the size suggested by the chart; but, what he had missed was the fine print, wording that stated "recommendations are for wind speeds less than 30-knots with moderate protection from seas and the boat having the freedom to oscillate". This storm had sustained winds of 50 knots, with gusts to over 70 knots, and where his boat had been anchored, there were many miles of fetch.

This small print is the crux of the problem. Even if present, this small print always seems to go unnoticed, and compounding the problem, there seems to be a dearth of information explaining how to size rope for rodes, snubbers, and dock lines, especially for when the conditions will worsen. Without this guidance, mariners are left to figure it out on their own, and as a result, many get it wrong.

-------------------------------------- § --

"If you cannot tie a knot, tie a lot."
From- *The Complete Rigger's Apprentice*

Seldom do ropes that are used for rodes, snubbers, and dock lines part due to lack of strength. Instead, they just about always chafe, which then allows them to part. This is a pervasive problem among boats. The question to ask is "why", and then, "can anything be done about it"? Fortunately, the answer is yes.

In their literature, Samson Rope, a rope manufacturer of worldwide renown, says, "normal Working Load Limits for rope are for ropes in good condition, with appropriate splices, in non-critical application, under normal service conditions and have not been subjected to dynamic loading". They go on to recommend that for 3-strand, 8-plait (brait), and 12-braid rope, 20 percent loading is the maximum for new, unused rope in non-critical situations.

The Cordage Institute, promulgators of the Standards to which member rope manufacturers must adhere, recommends that, "a rope with a Work Load Limit of 20 percent loading which makes its Design Factor only 5, should only be selected and used with expert knowledge of conditions and professional estimate of risk. Design Factors that are higher, 12:1 or more, should be used for severe service conditions". The key words that should jump out at the reader in these two paragraphs are *"non-critical", "normal",* and *"severe service",* as well as *"dynamic loading".*

50

Samson Rope points out some conditions which, for rope, would be considered "severe" service *(Italics are the author's remarks)*:

- Dynamic conditions, *which, for mariners, would include being anchored where the boat is subjected to seas, waves, or wind gusts;*
- Shock loads, *which, for mariners, would include insufficient cushioning of surge loads, non-judicial use of engine power with the anchor set, or setting the anchor while the boat has way on;*
- Non-appropriate splices, *which, for mariners, would include any poorly constructed splice, as well as an inappropriate splice for the job;*
- Extended service under load, *which, for mariners, would include anchoring for any duration in which the wind is strong enough to eliminate most or all of the rode's catenary;*
- Conditions where life, limb, or property is involved, *which, for mariners, is every time the boat is anchored, with this taking on more importance when the conditions turn harsh;*
- Exposure to elevated temperatures, *which, for mariners, would mean any stretch on the rope during conditions other than mild;*
- Excessive use, *which, for mariners, includes use of rope in high winds or heavy seas, or when the rope has exceeded its service life;*
- And, exposure of the rope to some chemicals, such as bleach, acids, and urine.

Even though every rope manufacturer asserts essentially these same stipulations, most mariners seem to be unaware of these warnings, or maybe they just choose to ignore them. Since anchoring in anything other than the mildest of conditions should be considered "severe", not "normal" service conditions, and the more severe the weather, the more "severe" the service, rope that is used for rodes, snubbers, and even dock lines, should have Work Load Limits compatible with this type of service.

To size rope for use as a rode, snubber, or dock line, and to get it "right", several interrelated characteristics of rope must be considered–stretch, length, strength, hand, material, and type of construction. These need to be balanced with one another, as well as with the use to which the rope will be subjected.

STRETCH

Stretch is that singularly touted characteristic that is frequently considered all-important in a rope rode or snubber. To a limited degree this is true, for without adequate stretch to cushion surge loads, the result is often broken or deformed gear. So, yes, stretch is important, but not at the expense of other, just-as-important characteristics that the rope must possess.

Another important point to understand is that rope used to cushion surge loads does not require the "most stretch possible", but only to have "enough stretch". How much is "enough"–at least 8 percent stretch at 15 percent loading.

LENGTH

This feature of rope is mostly self-evident; the rope must be long enough to accomplish its job, plus a little extra. But, in boating, there are a few "ropes" that seem to be consistently too short—mainly those used as snubbers, "docking lines", and dock lines.

A "snubber" is a line used to cushion surge loads, and as such it must have an adequate amount of "stretch length" in order for its "percentage of stretch" to be effective. For example, a rope with 10 percent stretch, but is only 10 feet long, will only stretch 1 foot, but the same rope, at

40 feet long, will stretch 4 feet, a marked improvement in this longer rope's ability to cushion surge loads.

Our opinion is, a snubber having at least 8 percent stretch at 15 percent loading, in order to provide enough stretch to adequately absorb surge loads, should be at least 30 feet long for gale force winds, and a minimum of 40 feet for storm conditions. But even longer rope, or rope with a higher percentage of stretch will do no harm and possibly do a lot of good.

A snubber of any of these lengths, in milder weather, can always be "snubbed shorter", with the advantage that it can be let out should the wind speed pick up.

"Docking lines" are those lines that are thrown, sometimes to folks on a pier, at other times around such things as a cleat, piling, or bollard. The simplest way to determine if a "docking line" is too short is to watch the results—are the folks on the dock having a hard time catching the line, or does the line not quite make it around the cleat or piling? If so, your "docking lines" need to be longer.

These lines, to be successful at their job, should not only be long enough to comfortably reach the object at which they are thrown, but they should also be long enough to extend many, many feet beyond the object. For many boats, this means that "docking lines" will need to be 30 feet in length, though for other boats, consistent success might not be achieved unless longer lines are thrown. Once the boat is secure in its slip or alongside the pier or quay, "docking lines", if of sufficient diameter, can be repositioned to act as "dock lines".

"Dock lines", lines that keep a boat fast in a slip or alongside a pier or quay, often cannot have the length necessary to allow for sufficient "stretch" in order to adequately cushion surge loads, since slips usually do not have the space that will allow for the use of long-enough lines. In slips that have good protection from wind or seas, this may be inconsequential, but not so in slips that are more exposed. So, many boaters instead use small diameter lines, thinking that they will work just fine. But, these small diameter lines, too, still do not have the length, and therefore the "stretch length", that is necessary to adequately cushion the surge loads once the wind picks up.

When these small diameter lines pull taut, the surge loads turn into shock loads, placing both the lines and their belaying points at risk for damage, including breakage. Worse still, these small diameter lines chafe easier than would larger diameter lines. Some mariners try to solve this problem of chafing by doubling up on these lines, but the result is just two small diameter lines that chafe.

> **TIP:** One approach to gain some extra "stretch length" in a "dock line" is to run the line through a strong-enough block, around the back of an item, such as a cleat or bollard, one in a location that will hold the boat in position, then, forming the largest obtuse angle possible, lead the line to and belay it at another point, one farther away. Another method is to run the line in what might be considered an opposite direction; e.g.- starboard stern line run to the port side, or a forward line run aft.

For "dock lines", to have increased resistance to chafe, it's best to use "large" diameter lines. Then, to get the stretch that is needed, add some mechanism that will allow for stretch, a common, lesser expensive product simply being a big, strong, black "stretchable band", usually called a "dock line snubber".

STRENGTH and SIZE

A rope used as a rode or snubber, just like all of the other components used in ground tackle, should have a Working Load Limit (WLL) that equals or exceeds the highest load that will be imposed on the ground tackle. However, this requirement is not as straightforward as it appears because rope does not come with a WLL, only tensile strengths are provided.

To deal with this issue, the American Boat and Yacht Council (ABYC) has set the standard that rope used in ground tackle should have a minimum Design Factor of 8. With this design factor, the maximum load on the rope will be 12.5 percent of the rope's tensile strength, giving rise to the moniker, the "12.5 percent" rule. But this does not reveal what size the rope needs to be, only how strong it needs to be.

> *To size rope for use in ground tackle, multiply the maximum load that will be on the ground tackle by 8 (the ABYC recommended Design Factor), thus establishing the tensile strength that the rope will need.*
>
> *Then, using the rope manufacturer's sizing chart, cross-reference this tensile strength to a size of rope that has this, or a greater tensile strength.*
>
>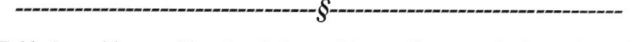
>
> **Table 5 provides an abbreviated chart of the tensile strengths for various sizes of rope.*

NON-CORDAGE INSTITUTE ROPE

Compliance with the Cordage Institute standards assures that the manufacturing process has adequate quality control and testing procedures in place in order to assure that the rope—when new—will meet the applicable standard for strength and diameter. Since compliance with the Cordage Institute standards is voluntary, some rope may not be manufactured so zealously, with the resultant rope's diameter or tensile strength being different from that found in the Cordage Institute standards. This issue, however, does not preclude the use of a non-Institute compliant rope. If non-Institute compliant rope is the choice, and as long as the rope's diameter is not critical for a particular application, since it is the rope's tensile strength that is important, not its size, the rope should be sized just as would be done for Institute-compliant rope, by identifying which size rope, based on data provided by its manufacturer, has the tensile strength needed. *(Cordage Institute membership list is available at www.ropecord.com/new/members.asp)*

SIZE vs STRETCH

When rope is sized in the manner suggested above, so that it is not loaded beyond 12.5 percent of its tensile strength, it's easy to assume that these sizes would have too little stretch to adequately cushion surge loads. Actually, just the opposite is true and this is a paradox that usually goes unrecognized (see Appendix 4). Three-strand, 8-plait (brait), and 12-braid Nylon ropes, at least those manufactured to the Cordage Institute standards, have at least 8 percent stretch at 15 percent loading, the

SPLICED BEFORE TESTED
Rope manufactured to Cordage Institute standards is tested for strength with eye splices in place. This protocol provides figures for tensile strength that more closely represents the use of rope in real life applications. Non-Institute compliant rope may not be tested for strength with eye splices in place. As a result, the figures for strength for non-Institute compliant rope may be higher in value than those for Institute compliant rope. To compare "apples-to-apples", so to speak, the loss of strength for a splice, if not already accounted for, should first be backed out of the non-Institute rope's figures prior to comparing them to figures for Institute-compliant rope. This value for loss of strength, due to a well-made eye-splice is typically 15 percent of the rope's tensile strength, but will be greater for poorly made splices.

minimum amount of stretch mentioned earlier in this chapter that is needed to adequately cushion surge loads. Some rope manufacturers produce rope with even more stretch than this which, if used, provides even better cushioning of surge loads.

56

APPROPRIATE LOADING FOR ROPE

It is readily apparent that rope can be loaded, without it breaking, beyond 12.5 percent of its tensile strength, the limit that is recommended by the ABYC. But with rope used in ground tackle, this is not the most important issue; the more important issue is how many load repetitions—cyclic loading—the rope can sustain, and how well the rope can resist chafe and melting. The issue of cyclic loading is even more significant considering the fact that ropes which are used as rodes, snubbers, and dock lines are constantly undergoing cyclic loading to one degree or another.

Research clearly shows that as the percentage of load on a rope increases, the number of load cycles to which the rope can be subjected, without breaking, decreases at an alarming rate. Then, add to this issue the increased ease with which chafe can occur as the percentage of load on a rope increases. Either of these two issues is a significant detriment to a rope used for rodes, snubbers, and dock lines, but to have both occurring simultaneously makes this issue of loading more than significant, it can be critical.

To put this information into practical use, if the percentage of load on the rope can be kept as low as possible, the number of load cycles that the rope will be able to sustain will significantly increase, while at the same time, the rope will be more resistant to chafe and melting. On the other hand, as the percentage of load increases, the less resistant the rope will be to chafe and melting and, due to cyclic loading, the sooner the rope will need to be replaced. This situation can be so severe that the rope, if it does not part during a bout of weather, will need to be replaced prior to its next use.

Making this issue even more dangerous is that the damage that is done to the rope is cumulative and permanent, often going unnoticed. Rope used under these circumstances, if it does not part during the episode in which the damage was done, often parts later with a load much less than the rope's rated load. Nope, if rope is going to be used in ground tackle, it is best to just to use rope that is sized to the "12.5 percent" rule.

SNUBBERS AND ROPE RODES

If the rode is all rope, or a combination rode (part rope and part chain), a snubber is not always necessary, if: 1) The rope is Nylon; 2) The rope is of an appropriate diameter; 3) The rope is made of 3-strand, 8-plait (brait), or 12-braid construction; and, 4) The rope portion is long enough, say a length of at least 40 feet.

But, even with rope rodes installing a snubber is good practice as, should anything chafe, better it be the snubber, leaving the rode healthy and thus able to continue to hold the vessel, at least for a time. As long as the nylon rope portion of the rode is long enough to provide adequate cushioning, say at least 40 feet in length, the snubber can be a short, hefty piece of rope, even made from low-stretch, higher-chafe resistant Dacron (polyester) rope.

HAND

Rope is manufactured by varying how tight the fibers are twisted together; the result is rope that can be extremely stiff, known as "hard laid," moderately stiff, known as "medium laid," or very un-stiff, known as "soft laid." The amount of stiffness is also called the rope's hand–a firm hand, medium hand or soft hand. Also manufactured, but less commonly found, are very hard-laid and very soft-laid ropes.

> **TIP:** To soften rope, just get it wet, though it is a very temporary solution; this works even with old or hard-laid line.

The harder the lay of the rope, the more chafe resistance it has, and

58

generally, the longer service life it will provide. While it may sound paradoxical, hard laid rope will also have more stretch than that of a softer lay. This is due to having more twist laid up in it during manufacturing, twist that untwists as the rope is tensioned.

On the other hand, hard laid rope will be fairly miserable to handle, will not flake down easily, and no amount of soaking in fabric softener will soften it. Soft-laid rope is just the opposite, and medium-laid rope falls in between.

MATERIAL

Today's rope choices can be mind-boggling: HMPE (Dyneema/Spectra), HMPP (Innegra-S), Aramid (Technora/Kevlar), LCP (Vectron), PBO (Zylon), Carbon Fibers, Polyester (Dacron), Polyamides (Nylon), Olefins (Polypropylene and Polyethylene), and a small assortment of natural fibers, like manila, hemp, and cotton.

Some of these materials have extreme strength with high cost, others have poor strength with low cost. Some chafe quickly, some have short service lives, and others are too slippery which makes it difficult for a knot or hitch to grip enough to hold well. Some might float, while others have almost no stretch. And if that's not enough, others exhibit too much creep, some will easily rot or degrade quickly when exposed to UV light or to chemicals; then, too, some are simply not readily available.

For every rope that exhibits one or more of these characteristics, there are others that exhibit just the opposite. What makes choosing rope even more confusing is that manufacturers will take two or more of these materials and combine them into one rope, trying to minimize a trait of one by the use of another material that has a different characteristic.

Fortunately, within this wide expanse of choices you can find a few materials suitable to be made into rope that can be used for rodes and snubbers. The one material that predominates in this arena is Nylon because it has good stretch, good strength, is cost effective, is easy to find, holds knots and splices well, resists UV light and most chemicals (not bleach, acids, or urine) and has a good service life when treated right.

For uses that need better resistance to chafe, polyester (Dacron) is a good choice. Polyester costs only slightly more than Nylon, but has much better chafe resistance. It also holds knots and splices well and has good resistance to UV light. Polyester rope, too, also gives good service life if treated right. But, on its own, it has too little stretch, so it's not well-suited for cushioning surge loads.

When dry, both Nylon and Dacron have about the same strength, but Nylon loses up to 15 percent of its strength when wet. To minimize this loss of strength due to wetness, some rope manufacturers use a coating on the fibers to reduce their ability to absorb water, effectively reducing the rope's loss of strength due to wetness to around 8 percent. This coating also usually improves the resistance of the rope to chafe.

On the other hand, these coatings break down, losing effectiveness. When choosing rope for use as an anchor rode or snubber, it is better to ignore any advantage given by these miracle products, as it is too difficult to establish when these coatings start to break down, therefore reducing any benefit that they may have imparted to the rope when it was new.

One advantage to sizing the rope that will be used as a rode, snubber, or dock line to the "12.5 percent rule" is that this idiosyncrasy of Nylon rope to lose strength as it gets wet is then rather a moot point, for even when wet, the rope still has 85 percent of its tensile strength remaining.

CONSTRUCTION

Three, Eight, Twelve, Single, or Double–when rope is manufactured, its fibers must be twisted or woven together, in other words constructed, and these figures relate to how the rope is constructed. Three-strand (twisted) construction is the least expensive, and has good chafe resistance, although it does not readily collapse on itself and attention must be paid to avoid kinking and hockling.

Eight-plait (brait) and 12-braid constructions also resist chafe well, cost only slightly more than 3-strand, collapse on themselves very well and are not as susceptible to kinking and hockling.

All three of these constructions, 3-strand, 8-plait, and 12-braid, if made of Nylon, usually have at least 8 percent stretch at 15 percent loading. With this amount of stretch any of these can be used for cushioning surge loads, as long as they are also of "long length" and are sized to the 12.5 percent rule.

Single braids are difficult, sometimes seemingly impossible to splice and have much less stretch than 3-strand, 8-plaited, or 12-braided ropes. Double braids are easy on the hands and readily collapse on themselves. But double braid lines have too little stretch for use as snubbers, are more expensive, in addition to being more complicated to splice, and also chafe much easier as compared to 3-strand, 8-plait, or 12-braid ropes.

KNOTS, BENDS, KINKS and HOCKLES

Tight radii are one of the down-falls of rope, weakening the rope, making it susceptible to parting at less than its rated load. For example, a knot weakens a rope more than does a splice, due to the fact that the rope's strands are bent to tighter radii in a knot, than in a splice. This weakness is not limited to just knots, bends, kinks, and hockles, this weakness is also present in rope going around other radii, such as sheaves, chocks, the boat's sheer, or hawse holes. The sharper the bend or the smaller the radius, the greater the strain on the outer fibers, the greater the wear and friction on the rope, thus the less load it takes to make the rope part.

EXTENDING SERVICE LIFE

To avoid shortening the service life of Nylon or polyester rope, or weakening it too much, Samson Rope offers the following suggestions for sizing bitts, Samson posts, fairleads, chocks, sheaves, or any other surface over which a Nylon or polyester rope might pass:

- When a rope is bending over an item, forming a static bend of less than 10 degrees, the diameter of the bend should be no less than 1.5 times the rope's diameter (or ½ of the rope's circumference).

- When a rope is bending over an item, forming a static bend greater than 10 degrees, the diameter of the bend should be no less than 3x the diameter of the rope.

- When a rope is bending over an item, forming a dynamic bend greater than 10 degrees, for a light load, the diameter of the bend should be no less than 4x the diameter of the rope; for a heavy load, with *braided rope*, the bend should be no less than 8x the diameter of the rope; though with *twisted or plaited rope*, the diameter of the bend should be no less than 10x the diameter of the rope. (HMPE should have a minimum bend radius of 8:1, but for Aramid, a minimum of 12:1 is recommended; for wire rope, it is a minimum of 20:1).

- When a rope will travel 180 degrees over a rolling sheave, the sheave diameter should be a minimum of 4x the rope's diameter. The sheave groove diameter should be no less than 10 percent greater than the rope diameter and be "U" shaped. The wider the angle formed by a rope as it bends over a sheave, the smaller the sheave can be. (HMPE and Aramid ropes should have a different sheave profile than that mentioned above, one with a more flattened profile.)

- For end-point terminations (bollards, Samson posts, or bitts), the diameter of all portions of the item that the line bends over should be at least 3x the diameter of the rope.

- A cleat's length should be at least 12x the diameter of the largest rope with which it will be used. If two lines will be made fast to the cleat, the cleat's length should be at least 16x the diameter of the largest rope used on it. The cleat should be through-bolted, with large backing pads.

The following will also affect the strength of Nylon or polyester rope:

- Bleach will cause a 30 percent loss of strength to the rope;

- Acids and Urine–human, fish, bird, or animal–will cause a 15 percent loss of strength to the rope;

- Age usually causes a loss of strength to the rope of 2 percent per year, even if the rope is kept in good condition;

- Knots will typically cause a loss of about 30 percent of the rope's strength, though there are some knots that will cause a greater loss;

- Splices typically cause a loss of about 15 percent of the rope's strength, though there are some or poorly made splices will result in a greater loss of strength.

MELTING TEMPERATURES

A rope's critical temperature point is that temperature at which the rope starts to become damaged, and the longer lasting or higher the temperature, the more the damage. This damage weakens rope, making it susceptible to parting at lower loads than that for which it is rated. The melting point is the temperature at which the rope's fibers immediately fail, either due to melting (oxidation) or molecular flow.

Nylon melts at 450°F, but its critical temperature is 325°F; polyester also melts at 450°F, but its critical temperature is 350°F; HMPEs (Dyneema/Spectra) melt at 300°F, but their critical temperature is only 150°F and Aramids (Technora/Kevlar) melt at 900°F, but their critical temperature is 520°F. These temperatures are easily reached when a rope that is heavily loaded, especially one that was sized to a low Design Factor, rubs against something, or the fibers within rub against each other, as occurs during repetitive stretching.

USED ROPE

The damage that occurs to rope is cumulative and permanent, often hidden. Even after examining a rope to assess its health, you should still seriously question whether it is prudent to buy it. An exception could be rope that, relative to its size, will not be subjected to heavy loads, and even then it might turn out to be a poor investment.

> **KEEP THE STRAIN OFF OF THE WINDLASS**
>
> Windlass mechanisms are seldom designed hefty enough to resist the high loads that can develop on a rode and do so without becoming damaged. Therefore the load should not be left on a wildcat or around a warping drum while the anchor is being set, the boat is lying to the anchor, or the anchor is being broken out. A snubber is an inexpensive way to remove the load from the windlass' mechanism and transfer the load to a strong point, one that is designed and installed to enable it to carry these loads. If cushioning surge loads is not the purpose of the snubber, the snubber can be a short length of hefty, non-stretchy rope. One of these short, hefty, non-stretchy snubbers is a practical and inexpensive alternative to a chain stopper.

ROPE AND WILDCATS

If a windlass' wildcat will be used to retrieve a rope rode, the rope must be sized to the wildcat, which means that for a rope/chain wildcat, the diameter of the rope will usually need to be twice that of the size of the chain; e.g., 3/8 inch chain will need 3/4 inch rope.

On the other hand, if the rode will be deployed and retrieved by hand, since there is no other requirement than that of the strands being able to fit through the chain's link, maybe a

> **TIP**: For those who have sailboats, but no windlass, a rope rode can often be lead aft to a winch, whether at the cockpit or, if strongly stepped, on the mast.

shackle, the rope can be sized to correspond to the ABYC recommendation of having a Design Factor of 8.

Since most rodes that run through a wildcat will also travel through a deck pipe into a rode locker, using rope that collapses on itself, such as 8-plait or 12-braid rope is an advantage.

A "chain-only" wildcat can often be used to retrieve rope, though the rope may need to be sized larger than the normal "twice-the-size-of-the-chain" standard used for rope/chain wildcats. If you are uncertain of the size of rope needed to work in your wildcat, a variety of 6-10 foot lengths of various diameter ropes could be trial-run first, under some tension, to discover which size will work best in the wildcat. But, keep in mind, as a load comes on the rode, the diameter of the rope, particularly with 12-braid, due to its "hollow" center, will compress some.

As for the deployment of a rope rode, wildcats, not having a retaining finger, particularly on a vertical windlass, may not consistently allow the windlass to deploy the rode without requiring assistance from the crew.

ROLLING HITCHES and SNUBBER BRAIDS

Snubbers (and bridles) can be attached easily and quickly to a rode, whether rope or chain, by using a rolling hitch, probably, at least

ROUND TURNS WITH
ROLLING HITCH

on a recreational boat, the most versatile knot in the entire repertoire of knots. If the diameter of the snubber is large enough to where the knot slips on the rode, this slippage can be eliminated by converting the end of the snubber into a "snubber braid".

SNUBBER BRAID

To make a "snubber braid", put a whipping around the snubber approximately 2 feet from its end, then un-lay the strands back to this whipping. If they are not already so, divide the strands into three equal bundles, then braid them back together like a girl does with her hair (Common Sinnet- Figure 2965 in *The Ashley Book of Knots)*. At the end of the braid, put on one or two whippings to hold everything together and trim any excess from the end. Attach the snubber braid to the rode, whether rope or chain, with a rolling hitch.

Putting a snubber braid in the end of a line is useful for other reasons also, such as with a line that is difficult to belay due to being hard-laid or having an end that is too stiff to be easily worked.

ONLY ONE RODE

It is possible to have only one size of rope rode, if: 1) It is sized for the highest load; 2) It is inspected often; and, 3) It is repaired or replaced immediately when there is a suspicion that it has been damaged. For mariners concerned that a rope of this size, in lighter conditions, will not adequately cushion surge loads, a variety of different diameter snubbers, all of long length, can be carried onboard and used in lower wind speeds.

EMERGENCY STOPPING

There are times when it is prudent to have an anchor ready for immediate deployment, such as for a last ditch effort to stop the boat after all else has failed. Instead of using chain on an emergency-braking anchor, it is better and often safer to use an all rope rode for the stretch it provides. This stretch will allow for cushioning should the emergency anchoring be done in rough conditions or if the boat will fetch up hard at the end of the rode's run.

> **LINE HANDLING COMFORT**
> To address the issue of comfort, when dealing with a heavily loaded line, it is generally accepted that half inch line is the smallest diameter line for handling comfort, if "comfort" can be the word to use.

If time allows, a turn or two, first taken around a Samson post, bitt, or a cleat before the rode is let to run will provide some measure of control, and snubbing the line as it goes out will lessen the ultimate total load on the line and belaying points as the boat is brought to a standstill. As with any rode, the bitter end should first be belayed on the boat prior to letting go the anchor. Since the loads that develop when the boat fetches up hard can be huge, be sure that the fittings that the turns are taken around, and to which the bitter end is belayed, are designed and installed to be beyond strong enough.

FLOATS

Floats can be used to mark the location of an anchor, being attached to the anchor by a pendant. When used for this purpose, since little or no strain comes on the pendant, the line can be of any diameter, even of a fairly small diameter. But, this line does need to be long enough for the float to remain on the surface at high tide, including any applicable storm surge, wave heights, and depths to which the anchor might bury.

When lines of this length are used in waters that are tidal, involving some mechanism, whether simple or expensive, to keep the line "gathered" is helpful. With the exception of the one idea in the side note, mentioning other methods for gathering the slack line is beyond the scope of this book.

TRIP LINES

Since a trip line may be called on to recover a fouled anchor, it must be of a diameter that is sufficient to handle the strain that can come on the line. This strain, even with anchors for a modest-size boat, can be in the many thousands of pounds, especially when the anchor is deeply buried.

When attaching a trip line to the anchor, the line must be attached to the back of the anchor–the crown–with the other end attached to the float. With this arrangement, as long as the trip line has not also fouled, the anchor can be pulled out backward. The bitter end can be arranged as follows:

- The line between the anchor and the float is left to float free, but should, for recovery, have enough length to allow the float-end of the line, when in the "deepest" water, to be brought up on the deck far enough to reach a belaying point. If not long enough, additional line will need to be bent on.

  > **TIP:** For both float and trip lines, there are a variety of fairly simple and inexpensive methods that can be used to gather the line, if it goes slack. As an example, one of the simplest is to lead the line through a loop that is attached to the float, which is then tied to a weight. As the water level lowers, the weight, pulling down, draws any slack through the loop. Experimentation with weight will lead to the appropriate amount required.

- Another approach is to attach the pendant's working end to the crown of the anchor, then run the pendant loosely back along the rode, the bitter end being made fast to the rode. This line should be long enough that, as the rode is recovered, the bitter end of this line is well within reach of the crew before the anchor has to come out of the bottom. If necessary, light lashings can be spaced at intervals along the line to snug the trip line up to the rode.

68

CAUTION USING FLOAT AND TRIP LINES

When you use a float line or a trip line, it can foul keels, props, rudders, or other appendages on your boat or another. If it happens, you must correct the problem at the earliest. If not, the risk includes the vessel dragging, tripping its anchor, or even breaking free.

NO LINES ON A BOAT?

As to the often-heard statement that "there are no ropes on a boat", Ashley writes, "There is an old saying that there are only seven ropes aboard a ship, but there are actually over sixty that have borne the name". Some of these "lines" are: man rope, bell rope, foot rope, bolt rope, tiller rope, buoy rope, bucket rope, clew rope, grab rope, tow rope, and wheel rope.

"LINE" VERSES "ROPE"

According to *Chapman- Piloting, Seamanship and Small Boat Handling*, "rope, once in use onboard a boat is called line, or by name of the rigging part it has become." Clifford Ashley, *in The Ashley Book of Knots*, mentions that "the word 'rope' is seldom heard on shipboard, where it generally refers to new stuff in unbroken coils". But, he also goes on to say that "rope is also the inclusive term applied to all cordage..." There are some subtle nuances within this last statement that allow for the interchange of these two words.

-- § --

Back to the boat which was mentioned at the beginning of this chapter. By risking that the rope he had chosen for his rode would be adequate, not only did this owner have to bear the cost involved in repairing the damage to his boat from the beaching, but he also had to pay quite a large sum of money to the company that he hired to get his boat off the shore and then to a boatyard. He also had to replace his ground tackle–the rode and anchor, plus all of the other components that were lost when the rode chafed through. In retrospect it's easy to see it would have been simpler, and less expensive to have used rope of a size equal to the conditions.

After this episode, the owner decided to outfit differently; he wanted to continue to use rope for his rodes, but once he knew better, saw the wisdom in sizing his new gear based on the maximum load that would be on his ground tackle. He focused on choosing rope of more appropriate sizes for the job, including any future conditions in which they would be used. In addition, this incident showed him the importance of using snubbers and good anti-chafe techniques, things he failed to employ prior to this incident.

EXAMPLES - CHAPTER 5

In this, and where applicable, in other chapters, examples, relevant to the chapter's topic, will be presented. These examples are based on a hypothetical 35 foot sailboat, modest in windage, anchored where it has moderate protection from seas, and with the freedom to oscillate.

In this chapter, the examples list the suggested sizes of rope for our hypothetical 35' sailboat. For the wind speeds that are used in this example, sizes for 3-strand, 8-plait, and 12-braid rope are shown for a maximum loading of 12.5 percent (Design Factor of 8). Sizes are based on the Cordage Institute standards. *(Twelve-braid rope has an 8 percent higher Minimum Breaking Strength than that of either 3-strand or 8-plait (brait) rope.)*

45-KNOT WINDS- 1800 lb. load on ground tackle
(1800 lbs. x DF 8 = requires a rope with 14,400 lb. tensile strength)

- 3-Strand Rope-   7/8 inch rope (17,280 lb. MBS)
- 8-Plait Rope-   7/8 inch rope (17,280 lb. MBS)
- 12-braid Rope-   7/8 inch rope (17,280 lb. MBS)

60-KNOT, SHORT DURATION WINDS- 3800 lbs. load on ground tackle
(3600 lbs. x DF 8 = requires a rope with 28,800 lb. tensile strength)

- 3-Stand Rope-   1 1/8 inch rope (28,260 lb. MBS)
- 8-Plait Rope-   1 1/8 inch rope (28,260 lb. MBS)
- 12-braid Rope-   1 1/8 inch rope (28,260 lb. MBS)

60-KNOT, LONG DURATION WINDS- Minimum Work Load Limit one size up from that required for 60-knot, short duration winds. If the rope is already significantly oversized for 60-knot, short duration winds, then no increase in size is required.*

- 3- Strand Rope-   1 1/4 inch rope (34,830 lb. MBS)
- 8-Plait Rope-   1 1/4 inch rope (34,830 lb. MBS)
- 12-braid Rope-   1 1/4 inch rope (34,830 lb. MBS)

*Throughout these examples, it is our thinking that, with the inclusion of the Safety Factor in the load tables, plus that of the rope, choosing a rope with a Work Load Limit that is "very, very slightly" less than the load found in any of these tables will not, at least in any appreciable manner, increase the risk of the item failing.

CHAPTER 6

ANCHORS–SIZING & STRENGTH

It was a beautiful, balmy 4th of July in the Florida Keys. It seemed like everyone in the area who had a boat was out on the water to watch the fireworks. Laughing, drinking and generally a fun time for all… until the squall blew through. During the squall, a good number of the boats, big and little, dragged, several turned over and a few folks lost their lives. Yes, for some, inadequate scope contributed to this catastrophe, but for others, it was their anchor that was the culprit.

This incident highlights the importance for an anchor to be of adequate size, a suitable design for the bottom, and deployed appropriately, not only for the conditions at the time, but also with an eye towards the future.

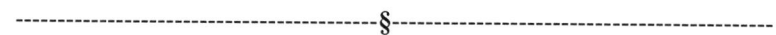

**"An anchor does not have to outperform another anchor,
it only has to outperform Mother Nature."**

"POOR HOLDING"- How many times has that thought been voiced or written about an anchorage? Well, maybe after reading this chapter, you might start viewing statements like this with a more critical eye. From our experience, we seldom find places that have "poor holding", though we often find places where the boaters are using the wrong anchors, or are employing the wrong techniques.

One exception is where the bottom is comprised of rock, maybe covered with a thin layer of soil. But, in anchorages with other types of bottoms, there is hope for boaters who wish to put down a "hook" and not drag, even in bottoms that are considered more of a challenge.

When it comes to choosing an anchor, whether to buy one, or every time you go to use it, several factors must be weighed: design, size, holding power, strength, ability to set on its own, plus any specific weakness, liability, or idiosyncrasy of the design which would cause it to not set, or to drag, trip, or break free.

Most mariners are aware that when the size of the boat gets bigger, beamier, or the wind speed rises, the anchor must be bigger. But, two other factors that are seldom taken into account also influence the size of the anchor needed: the bottom's composition and the anchor's fluke angle.

BOTTOM COMPOSITION

Although scientists can break soil into a seemingly endless number of categories, we will keep it as simple as is practical, limiting the choices to the types of bottoms recreational boaters are most likely to encounter. From R.S. Crenshaw, Jr., Naval Shiphandling, (Annapolis, MD: Naval Institute Press, 1975), the following is a list of the coefficients for various types of soils, each in comparison to firm sand:

Stiff, dense clay- 1.5 the resistance of sand
Firm sand- 1
Sticky clay- .66 the resistance of sand
Soft mud- .33 the resistance of sand
Coarse, loose sand- .33 the resistance of sand
Gravel- .33 the resistance of sand
Hard (rock) **bottom- 0**

These bottoms can be mixed, or contain shells, rocks, or weeds.

The one point that should be taken from these figures and is most important to understand, is this: regardless of anchor design, the softer (or looser) the bottom, the larger the anchor will need to be to have the same holding power as it would in firm sand.

However, there is a caution that applies: Although the composition of the bottom is important in the decision as to which design and size of anchor to use, it is the actual layer in which the anchor will set that must be used to make these decisions. If the composition of this layer differs from that of a superficial top layer, and the choice is made based on the top layer, poor setting or poor holding often results. Not only should a crew be cognizant that bottoms like this exist, these multi-layered types of bottoms can cause findings from an "anchor test" to appear to be different or conflicting with those from other tests.

FLUKE ANGLE

An anchor's fluke-to-shank angle, or "fluke angle", also has a great influence on an anchor's holding power, and when it comes to sizing an anchor, fluke angles cannot be ignored.

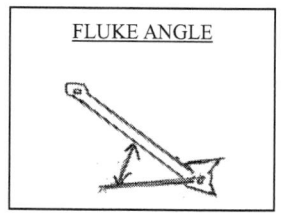
FLUKE ANGLE

For stock-stabilized, pivoting-fluke anchors, such as Danforth and Fortress anchors, a 32-degree fluke angle, *in sand,* is necessary for the anchor to develop its highest holding, but *in mud,* a 45-degree fluke angle maximizes the anchor's holding power. Change these angles and the anchor's holding power changes... for the worst.

For example, a stock-stabilized, pivoting fluke anchor with a 32-degree fluke angle, in mud, will typically have, depending on how soft the bottom is, $1/3^{rd}$ to $1/6^{th}$ the holding power that it would have in sand, while the same design in sand, but with a 45-degree fluke angle, will often have difficulty setting, and if it does set, it will hold poorly, if at all.

This is true for all anchors; since most anchors are designed to excel in a particular type of bottom, their use in other types of bottoms will more than likely show less than optimum holding power. If the anchor was designed with a "compromise" fluke angle, its holding power in all types of bottoms also will be a compromise.

These two rules are so important they bear repeating:
1) The softer the bottom, the larger the larger the anchor needed.
2) An anchor with an ineffective fluke angle needs to be even larger.

Frequently debated, often heatedly, is the topic of which anchor is better than another, but any argument put forth pales in comparison to the question of whether the anchors are big enough to begin with.

Should any recommendation for an anchor's size not include allowances for a soft (or loose) bottom or, if present, an ineffective fluke angle, or if the forces acting on the boat will be greater than that on which the recommendation was based, more than likely, no matter which anchor design is chosen, it will fail to hold adequately. Compounding this problem is that adequate guidance is seldom provided for up-sizing anchors.

As stated at the beginning of this chapter, the goal is not to pick an anchor that can out-perform another anchor, but instead to pick an anchor that can out-perform Mother Nature.

SIZING ANCHORS

For their designs, the anchor's manufacturer can often help in the

76

choice of an appropriately sized anchor for a particular size boat. But, caution is needed, as many times a recommendation may have neglected to factor in higher wind speeds, the boat's windage, the degree of exposure to seas, duration of the weather, or other factors that contribute to the load on the ground tackle. Nor may the recommendations take into account the softness of the bottom in which the anchor will be used, or the effectiveness of the anchor's fluke angle in that bottom.

SIZING CHARTS

Just about every anchor manufacturer provides a chart indicating the anchor size needed for a corresponding boat size. However, you should understand that the recommendations are often for the anchor's *use in sand, in winds of less than 30-knots, where there is moderate protection from seas, and with the boat free to oscillate.* Therefore, the recommendations from these charts are not of much benefit should the boat be anchored in soft bottoms, in winds close to or greater than 30-knots, where there is little protection from seas, or if the boat is anchored fore and aft. In other words, charts like these are a starting point for sizing your anchor, nothing more.

ANOTHER SIZING OPTION

Since fluke angles of 32-degrees or 45-degrees are not used in every anchor design, for this discussion we'll use the terms "shallow angle" (best suited for sand) and "deep angle" (best suited for mud).

Examples of shallow-fluke angle anchors are: stock-stabilized, pivoting fluke anchors like Danforth and Guardian, along with other fixed-fluke anchors, designs like the Plow, Claw, and scoop anchors, or adjustable anchors like the Fortress FX series, and the Super MAX anchor, when these latter two anchors are adjusted to their shallow angle setting. Examples of deep-fluke angle anchors are the Navy Stockless designs, or adjustable fluke anchors, when adjusted to their deep angle setting.

The following recommendations have proved sound for sizing anchors using an anchor manufacturer's chart as a baseline, as long as the chart recommendations are based on no less than 30-knots of wind, with the boat having moderate protection from seas, being anchored in sand, and having the freedom to oscillate.

Should the anchor you want have less fluke area than is typical for other similar poundage anchors, the anchor should be up-sized from that suggested below.

IN SANDY BOTTOMS, FOR A SHALLOW-FLUKE ANGLED ANCHOR:

- For winds up to 25-knots, no increase in size;
- For 25-45 knot winds, go up at least one size;
- For 45-60 knot winds, go up at least two sizes.

IN SANDY BOTTOMS, FOR A DEEP-FLUKE ANGLED ANCHOR:

- Anchors with a deep fluke angle, regardless of size, will usually set and hold unreliably and are best not used in sand. Fisherman-style anchors are the exceptions to this rule.

IN SOFT (OR LOOSE) BOTTOMS, FOR A DEEP-FLUKE ANGLED ANCHOR:

- For winds up to 25-knots, go up at least one size;
- For 25-45 knot winds, go up at least two sizes;
- For 45-60 knot winds, go up at least three sizes.

IN SOFT (OR LOOSE) BOTTOMS, FOR A SHALLOW-FLUKE ANGLED ANCHOR:

- For winds up to 25-knots, go up at least two sizes;

- For 25-45 knot winds, go up at least three sizes;

- For 45-60 knot winds, go up at least four sizes, and if the mud is very soft, go up at least five sizes.

FISHERMAN-STYLE ANCHORS: These anchors, if they have moderate size palms and are made to traditional-dimensions, like the Luke or Kingston anchors, are sized by weight:

- For winds up to 25-knots, in sand- 1 lb. of anchor per foot of boat length, or for soft (or loose) bottoms, 1.5 lb. of anchor per foot of boat length;

- For 25-45 knot winds, in sand- 1.5 lbs. of anchor per foot of boat length, or for soft (or loose) bottoms, 2 lbs. of anchor per foot of boat length;

- For 45-60 knot winds, in sand- 2 lbs. of anchor per foot of boat length, or for soft (or loose) bottoms, 2.5-3 lbs. of anchor per foot of boat length.

TENSILE STRENGTH

Although tensile strength, the strength to resist bending or breaking, is often thought to be related to holding power, it is not the same thing, and just because an anchor has plenty of one, does not mean that there is enough of the other. An anchor that might have adequate holding power may need to be up-sized in

> **BENT ANCHORS**
> An anchor, once bent, is unreliable and must be straightened to its original shape to function as originally designed. If an anchor can be straightened, most machine shops, even some welders, should be able to do so. For take-apart anchors, if the design has a particular piece that is known for bending or breaking, or being dropped overboard, it's a good idea to keep one or more of these pieces on hand for quick replacement. If an anchor cannot be returned to its original shape, it must be relegated to employment as a door stop or garden ornament.

order to provide adequate strength, and vice versa.

When manufacturers publish the tensile strengths of their anchors, these figures can be used to identify the size of anchor that will have enough strength to exceed, ideally, by a factor of 4, the maximum load that is calculated for the ground tackle. Unfortunately, many manufacturers do not publish this data; in these cases, a call to the manufacturer may elicit this specific information. For those manufacturers who do not, it is our opinion that they should start doing so.

Often our eyes alone can provide the evidence needed to disregard a particular size of anchor, and evidence like this should not be disregarded lightly. In other words, if an anchor is deformed, this is prima facie evidence that this particular size of anchor did not have the strength needed for the conditions in which the deformation occurred. To use this same design in similar conditions, a bigger anchor, one with more strength is needed.

Anchors should also have the strength necessary to resist side (bending) loads, though not all designs can, or even should attempt to reach this lofty goal. If circumstances require the use of an anchor that is not hefty enough to resist bending loads, and these bending loads cannot be avoided, about the only other option available, and one that should be used, is to deploy multiple anchors in a pattern that would prevent the entire load on the ground tackle from being imposed on any one anchor in such a way that any one of the anchors will deform or break (see Appendix 7).

ADDITIONAL THOUGHTS:

- International Classification Societies recommend that an anchor's holding power be twice that of the maximum load expected to be on the anchor. Sizing an anchor's holding power in this way provides some tolerance for errors when calculating for the anticipated load, but even so, errors should not be intentionally introduced into these calculations. This statement, taken by itself, however, is deceptive, as the anchor needs to be sized to have this amount of holding power in the softest bottom that will be encountered.

- Recommendations for an anchor's size should be considered as the smallest size to be chosen, not the largest. If ever in doubt, choose a bigger anchor, and if given a choice, choose a much-bigger anchor;

- For comparable holding power, designs that have less fluke area will need to be bigger than those with greater fluke area;

- Every anchor has only a maximum amount of holding power; if more holding power is required, a larger anchor or a different design is needed;

> **CAN AN ANCHOR BE TOO BIG?**
> With a few caveats, for most general purpose anchors we think not, and here's why. If the boat's not moving neither is the anchor, so there is no dragging. If the anchor does start to drag, the anchor will set itself, but only if: 1) the anchor design is appropriate to the type of bottom in which it is being used, and 2) the anchor has the ability to set with the amount of rode (scope) that has been deployed.

- No matter how big, how heavy, how awkward to handle, or how expensive the anchor might be, it is counterproductive to under-size an anchor because of any of these factors.

- A single anchor, tandem anchors, or multiple anchors can become fouled in shifting currents or winds. But debris in the water, or other causes, can also foul anchors. Once fouled, the odds increase dramatically that the anchor(s) will drag or trip or that the boat will break free. The longer deployed, the greater the risk. All anchors need to be pulled periodically, inspected, then reset; the frequency of inspection is dependent on the circumstances and environment.

ABILITY TO RESET

Once an anchor trips, the question then is, will it reset? The most common causes for an anchor to not reset are: clogging, jamming, deformation, insufficient sea room, or insufficient time.

If an anchor trips, a wise captain pulls the anchor back to the surface in order to check for and correct any reason that would interfere with its ability to reset, and if necessary, switch the anchor out for another, one better suited to the conditions.

Also, some anchors cannot reset if too much scope is deployed. If this is the case, shorten the rode in order to get the anchor to reset, then, once reset, let out enough rode that the anchor will have adequate holding power (see Chapter 8). For a hard bottom, one in which longer than normal scopes were needed to get the anchor to set (see Chapter 7), to reset the anchor, longer than normal scopes may again be needed.

The alternative to risking having your anchor trip, and one that you should be very willing to pursue from the very first, is to deploy multiple anchors in a pattern that would prevent enough of a load on any one anchor that would cause it to trip (see Appendix 7).

You should take note that the purpose of deploying more than one anchor is to prevent any one anchor from tripping, not to catch the boat after one trips. This is a subtle distinction, but an important one, since, if one anchor trips, so might the other(s).

"THE BIG 5"

As we pointed out in the Introduction, an anchor's design and size are only two of the five factors needed to prevent a boat from breaking free or dragging. The other three are: strength of all of the components, adequate scope, and appropriate anti-chafe techniques. We cannot emphasize enough that each, not just some, of these "Big 5" meet the minimum requirements, requirements that are set by Mother Nature, not by us. And when necessary, do not forget about the need to deploy more than one anchor. Remember, "this is not a speed sport, nor is it for the lazy".

SMALLER ANCHORS

Once you have anchors onboard that are suitable for the most demanding conditions that the boat will encounter is it appropriate to consider smaller anchors, those sized for less severe conditions or for convenience. However, if money is tight or stowage space is limited, smaller anchors may not be necessary since "large-enough-for-storms" anchors and their associated gear can also be used in lesser conditions.

HOW MANY ANCHORS ARE NEEDED

With the exception of when boating in small farm ponds, having no anchor, even for a dinghy or small boat, is just plain lubberly. Good seamanship demands having onboard at least one complete set of ground tackle sized for the heaviest weather while anchored in the softest (loosest) bottom, or, if you encounter them, weeds. That, and the equipment needed, along with any necessary arrangements to deploy and retrieve it.

But, sizing ground tackle can present a dilemma for a mariner. Size your ground tackle for severe conditions and it will be bigger, stronger, heavier, and more costly than you need for more typical conditions. But size your ground tackle for typical conditions and it will be inadequate when the conditions become more severe. So what is a mariner to do?

There are at least a couple of solutions. One is to have one set of ground tackle, the main bower, sized, say, for up to 45-knot winds, a wind speed that is frequently experienced with those quick appearing squalls or those nighttime thunder(less) storms that often show up unannounced. Then, another set, the storm anchor, and all of its associated gear, sized for more severe conditions, say, 60-knot winds.

One problem with this approach, and it can be a big problem, occurs with the appearance of winds that are higher than 45-knots and there is no opportunity to change out the main bower for the heftier storm gear.

To avoid such a situation, another approach is to size the main bower, and all of its associated gear for 60-knot winds. With this approach the main bower will then be able to handle short-duration, severe conditions that show up unexpectedly.

In addition to this main bower, a second set of ground tackle, the "storm anchor" and all of its associated gear, should also be onboard. This storm gear should be sized for long-duration, 60-knot winds. This means that this gear, all of it, will need to be heftier than that of the main bower, since long duration conditions are harder on the gear than are wind speeds of the same level, but of shorter duration.

This latter approach is particularly well-suited, not only for vessels that will range farther afield, but also for those who leave their boat or go to sleep while the boat is anchored, or for any other reason, are not able to switch out their ground tackle in a timely manner.

In addition, having this "storm gear" aboard can allow it to be used as a second anchor, or to replace the main bower if it has been slipped or lost. Most importantly, as long as this gear is suitable for the type of bottom in which it will be used, it can be used anytime that the main bower's ability to hold is doubtful. This reason alone is an excellent reason for having shipped a big-enough, all-purpose anchor, such as a fisherman-style anchor.

For boats in hurricane prone areas, enough anchors and their associated gear sized for hurricane force winds should also be on hand. As

84

long as such gear is available in a timely manner, it does not need to be stowed on the boat.

But the above recommendations still may not be sufficient. For anchorages where the wind shifts or the current reverses direction, good seamanship demands a minimum of two sets of ground tackle onboard, each capable of holding the boat in the severest conditions and softest bottom (or weeds) encountered. Deciding whether to deploy both sets, or just one, depends on the circumstances.

NOT ENOUGH ANCHORS

If you are caught in shifting winds or currents and don't have enough anchors to lay out in order to deal with the entire shift, all is not lost. One solution is to reposition the available anchor(s) to counter the upcoming changes. The big problem is that you will likely be repositioning anchors every few hours, either from the boat or by getting in the water. Yes, this will need to continue until the conditions no longer require it, and must be done regardless of whether it is inopportune to do so. It is just much easier and simpler to have onboard an adequate number of anchors that are big enough and are specific for the type of bottom to begin with.

MORE THAN TWO ANCHORS?

Three sets of ground tackle, each capable of holding the boat in the severest conditions and in the softest bottom (or weeds) encountered, may be necessary, especially when anchoring where the swing room will not allow lying to fewer anchors. There may be other compelling reasons to have at least this number of anchors onboard.

AFTER ALL IS SAID AND DONE

It's seldom, if ever, a problem if you have the appropriate gear and it isn't needed, but unfortunately, the opposite situation, where the gear is needed, but isn't onboard, is just about always trouble.

EXAMPLES - CHAPTER 6

In this, and where applicable, in other chapters, examples, relevant to the chapter's topic, will be presented. All of the examples will be based on a hypothetical 35 foot sailboat, modest in windage, anchored where it has moderate protection from seas and with the freedom to oscillate.

In this chapter, the examples will be for sizing anchors for our 35' hypothetical sailboat, by:

- Using a generic sizing chart.
- Using a manufacturer's chart.
- Sizing Fisherman-style anchors.

GENERIC SIZING CHART IN WHICH THE ANCHOR SIZES INCREASE IN APPROXIMATELY 10 POUND INCREMENTS:

SAND (shallow fluke angle)

- Up to 45-knot winds-   45 lb. anchor
- Up to 60-knot, short duration winds-   55 lb. anchor
- Up to 60-knot, long duration winds-   65 lb. anchor

SAND (deep fluke angle)

- Poor setting and poor holding would be expected; this fluke angle is not recommended for use in sand.

MUD (shallow fluke angle)

- Up to 45-knot winds-   65 lb. anchor
- Up to 60-knot, short duration winds-   75-85 lb. anchor
- Up to 60-knot, long duration winds-   85-95 lb. anchor

MUD (deep fluke angle)

- Up to 45-knot winds-   55 lb. anchor

- Up to 60-knot, short duration winds-   65 lb. anchor
- Up to 60-knot, long duration winds-   75-85 lb. anchor

ANCHORS WITH HOLDING POWER DATA PROVIDED BY THE MANUFACTURER- Fortress Anchors are used in this example. (*MHP= Minimum Holding Power*):

SAND (32-degree fluke angle):

- 45-knot winds-   1800 lbs. MHP required- FX-7
- 60-knot, short duration winds-   3800 lbs. MHP required- FX-16
- 60-knot, long duration winds-   3800+ lbs. MHP required- FX-23

MUD (32-degree fluke angle):

- 45-knot winds-   1800 lbs. MHP required- FX-37
- 60-knot, short duration winds-   3800 lbs. MHP required- FX-125
- 60-knot, long duration winds-   3800+ lbs. MHP required- FX-125

MUD (45-degree fluke angle):

- 45-knot winds-   1800 lbs. MHP required- FX-23
- 60-knot, short duration winds-   3800 lbs. MHP required- FX-55
- 60-knot, long duration winds-   3800+ lbs. MHP required-FX-55

FISHERMAN-STYLE ANCHORS:

SAND

- up to 45-knot winds-   55 lb. anchor
- up to 60-knot, short duration winds-   70 lb. anchor
- up to 60-knot, long duration winds-   80-90 lb. anchor

MUD

- up to 45-knot winds-   70 lb. anchor
- up to 60-knot, short duration winds-   90 lb. anchor

- up to 60-knot, long duration winds-   100 lb. anchor

CHAPTER 7

SEABEDS & ANCHOR DESIGNS

It was winter in the Bahamas, the Abacos to be more precise, and on this particular day the winds were forecast to reach into upper gale force levels by midnight. We were anchored in a small cove when a 60-foot schooner powered in and dropped anchor. Boy was that schooner handsome—traditionally built, long, lean, miles of rigging—with a large fisherman anchor catted-off at the bow.

However, instead of dropping that fisherman anchor in this sandy bottom that was densely covered with turtle grass, the schooner deployed two contemporary anchors from bow rollers, a large plow and a large Bruce, both on heavy chain rodes.

Later, on our way to the dinghy dock, as we rowed over them, we could see through the clear water that this schooner's anchors were not dug in. Instead, this schooner was being held in place only by the friction of the anchors and chain lying on top of the weeds, what we call being "ground-tied".

While ashore, we said hello to a fella who turned out to be the captain of that schooner. After some pleasantries, we expressed our surprise in his choice of anchors. We can quote his response, as even today, 15 years later, it stands out in our minds, "That boat ain't goin' anywhere. I've got over 400 lbs. of gear sitting on the bottom and the boat didn't budge when I backed down."

Okay, we thought, who are we to question the way that this captain runs his boat. More importantly, at least to us, this schooner was anchored behind us and the wind was not forecast to clock around.

Then, at 0200, we were awakened by that distinctive sound of clattering chain, accompanied by a lot of yelling, coming from the schooner. Yep, the wind did live up to expectations, but that schooner's 400 lbs. of ground tackle that was just lying on the bottom did not.

-------------------------------------- § --------------------------------------

**"Anchors should be chosen based on what they can do.
But, they should be used in a manner based on what they cannot do."**

ANCHOR DESIGN KEY POINTS:

- An anchor's design is important but it does not stand alone; the anchor must also have adequate size for the type of bottom and have enough strength for the conditions (see Chapter 6).

- Subtle differences between anchors that look "alike" can result in significant differences in performance.

- Different anchor designs of similar weights do not necessarily have similar holding power.

- The design must be able to set on its own, in the type of bottom in which it will be used; diving on the anchor to set it may not be practical or even possible.

- Any anchor under the right circumstances can trip, though some anchors are thought to be more inclined to do so than others.

> **TRIPPING**
>
> The causes for an anchor tripping are many and varied, but the following seem to predominate:
> - The anchor being too small for the circumstances;
> - The anchor became jammed, clogged, or fouled;
> - Inadequate scope;
> - The boat veered before the anchor set deep enough.

90

Regardless of which anchor design is being used, when the possibility of tripping is present, one or more additional anchors should be deployed in a manner that will prevent any one of the anchors from tripping (see Appendix 7).

- In addition to preventing tripping, deploying more than one anchor should also be considered when there is: 1) a need to limit the boat's swing room; 2) a possibility that the load on the ground tackle might be enough to bend the anchor; or, 3) a risk of rode wrap, whether around its own anchor or some other object.

> **THE INFLUENCE OF SCOPE ON THE ANCHOR'S DEPTH OF BURY**
>
> For maximum holding power, as the load develops on the anchor, the anchor must be able to get far enough down into dense-enough layers. Even with boats in the mid-thirty foot range in winds of gale force level, when anchoring in soft bottoms, this can require that the anchor bury more than ten feet. If burying depth is not included in your scope calculation, a too-short rode can restrict your anchor's ability to bury deep enough, which will limit the anchor's ability to develop its maximum holding power in that bottom.

- Regardless of design, good deployment technique is important in getting an anchor to set; the softer the bottom, the more important this becomes (see Chapter 14).

- Anchors or other gear and techniques which may be successful in harsh conditions that are short-lived, may not be adequate in more prolonged conditions.

SEABEDS

In this chapter, the terms "shallow" and "deep" fluke angles, as defined in Chapter 6, are used.

STIFF, DENSE CLAY or HARD MARL

91

For stiff, dense clay, hard marl, or other hard bottoms (not "rock" bottoms), an anchor should have a "shallow" fluke angle, sharp edges, and being heavy seems to be an advantage. If the edges of an anchor are dull, a welder or machine shop can usually sharpen them. It is also possible to sharpen them yourself using an angle grinder and metal files.

If the anchor, during the attempt to set it, catches and releases or just skips over the bottom, to encourage the flukes to dig in, the shank should be kept as low as possible, which usually can be accomplished by using longer scopes, 5:1, 7:1, or possibly more. Also, the "pull and pause" technique, explained later in this chapter, can sometimes be helpful to get the anchor to set in bottoms like this.

Another idiosyncrasy of anchoring in bottoms like this is that the anchor often sets shallow, enough so that it is susceptible to pulling out or tripping should the wind or current shift. This risk is exacerbated if the speed of the wind

> **TIP:** When anchored in boulders, hard clay, hard marl, or any other type of bottom in which the anchor's hold can be tenuous, a wise captain sets and maintains an anchor watch.

rises. The use of multiple anchors for conditions like this should be considered (see Appendix 7).

Size the anchor as shown in Chapter 6 for firm sand.

FIRM SAND

Nearly any anchor with a "shallow" fluke angle will set well in firm sand. Conversely, anchors with a "deep" fluke angle, which are designed for use in soft bottoms, perform poorly in sand, often not digging in at all. If they do set, they most likely will not develop high holding power.

Size the anchor as shown in Chapter 6 for firm sand.

STICKY CLAY or SOFT MARL

Just about any anchor with a "shallow" fluke angle can set in sticky clay or soft marl. As with firm sand, anchors with a "deep" fluke angle perform poorly in this type of bottom.

Size the anchor as shown in Chapter 6 for mud.

MUD

Mud and other soft bottoms can be most perplexing for anchoring. These bottoms run the gamut from dense and thick, to loose and silty. And, herein lies the problem. Without prior experience in a particular spot, most likely you'll be uncertain of which of these compositions you're dealing with. Fortunately, just about any anchor that can set in sand can also set in mud, although, and this is a huge "although", the anchor will need to be bigger to have the same holding power in the mud as it would have in sand.

In mud, an anchor with a deep fluke angle will develop more holding power than the same size design with a shallow fluke angle, though the anchor still may not have sufficient holding power unless it is also up-sized.

Not only does mud require an anchor that is bigger for the same holding power you would have in sand, but as the mud gets softer, the anchor has to be even bigger. If you have any doubt about the consistency of the mud that you will be anchoring in, size the anchor for soft mud, maybe even very soft mud.

Anchoring in mud requires not only a larger anchor but good deployment technique. We saw this repeatedly in the 2014 anchor test where the anchors that were being tested in the Chesapeake Bay mud were essentially just dropped overboard. During the four day testing period, most every anchor had an occasion when it just would not set. One hypothesis put forth was that, with no opportunity to orient themselves properly to the bottom, the anchors could not set; instead, they were just pulled, probably upside down, along on top of the seabed, flying, skating, or planning, definitely not digging in or setting.

Based on what we observed in that testing, the anchors that appear to be the least influenced by poor deployment technique are those which have proportionally more weight in their tips; the Spade anchor was one. From our personal experiences, as well as those of other folks, the Super MAX anchor also sets well in mud regardless of how it lands on the bottom.

Anchors that depend on a structural member, such as a roll bar or tipping palms to orient for proper setting, set much less reliably in mud. The softer the mud, the more likely it is that structural appendages will fail to perform, especially if coupled with poor deployment technique. The problem, we believe, is this: in mud these structural appendages have nothing firm enough to "push" against to force the anchor into its proper orientation to be able to set in the bottom.

So when anchors are used in soft bottoms, good anchor deployment technique, along with dealing with any idiosyncrasies a particular design might have is a particularly important role in getting them the anchors to set. For a discussion on helpful techniques to use for setting anchors in mud, see the end of this chapter.

Size the anchor as shown in Chapter 6 for mud.

COARSE, LOOSE SAND

Almost any anchor with a "shallow" fluke angle can be set in coarse, loose sand. Anchors with a "deep" fluke angle will set or hold poorly, if at all, in a bottom like this.

While for coarse, loose sand the anchor does not have to be quite as large as one for soft mud, it probably should be bigger than one used in firm sand.

Size the anchor as shown in Chapter 6 for mud.

PEBBLES AND GRAVEL (ROCKS or ROCKY BOTTOM)

Pebbles and gravel act like ball-bearings, allowing an anchor to slide through them. To develop adequate holding power, an anchor used in these bottoms needs more fluke area than one used in sand. Plus, in rocks, as in mud, the anchor also needs to bury far enough down to develop enough holding power. This is another type of bottom wherein scrimping on scope may prevent the anchor from burying as deep as it might need to in order to develop its full holding potential.

In this type of bottom, an anchor with small tolerances between parts, moving or otherwise, often becomes clogged or obstructed, preventing the anchor from working properly unless the anchor is first cleared.

Size the anchor as shown in Chapter 6 for mud.

BOULDERS

To set an anchor in an area strewn with boulders, the anchor has to become jammed between boulders, or if big enough, the anchor might be able to "wrap" around a proportionally sized boulder. But, if the boulder's purchase on the bottom is tenuous, so is the anchor's hold. Even if the boulder is strongly secured to the seabed, the anchor's purchase on the boulder, in and of itself, can be tenuous enough that it can lose its grip, especially if the boat veers even a little.

> **ANCHOR ALARMS**
> There are a variety of anchor alarms that can be utilized, from the simplistic—a weight lying on the seabed tied by light line to one's toe, or to a can filled with rocks—to the latest in contemporary electronics. But none substitute for having the appropriate ground tackle onboard, and using it appropriately as the circumstances dictate.

Since it is often difficult or impossible to retrieve an anchor that has fouled in a bottom like this, prior to deploying it, scow the anchor (see

95

Appendix 6), or install a trip line (Chapter 5).

Size anchors to have adequate strength to resist bending loads.

WEEDS

Weeds, a general term for grass, kelp, or other vegetation, can grow in most any of the seabeds listed above. Coverage can range from sparse to dense, while the weeds themselves can range from long, tough, or fibrous to short, "weak", or stringy. Any of this growth can be slippery enough that most anchors will just slide along on top of the weeds.

At one end of the spectrum, where the weed growth is sparse, any anchor suitable for the type of bottom in which the weeds are growing will usually set, since the anchor will most likely be digging into the seabed itself, not in the weeds.

On the other hand, in dense, long, tough, fibrous, slippery, or other difficult-to-penetrate growth, most anchors have difficulty setting, seldom, if ever, reaching through weeds or their roots to reach into the actual sea bottom. This is problematic

> **ANCHORING IN WEEDS**
>
> Often the following suggestions are offered for anchoring in weeds: 1) look for a spot devoid of weeds and drop the anchor in it; or, 2) go down and set the anchor by hand; but...
>
> - If the anchor cannot set on its own, even with the crew's involvement, what would allow it to reset if it trips, especially if it then drags out of that bare spot and into the weeds?
> - What if there is no spot devoid of weeds?
> - What if it is too dark, too deep, too cold, there is too much current, or the conditions are too dangerous to dive on the anchor?
> - What if you cannot swim or hold your breath long enough?
> - What if it is not possible to push the anchor through the weeds and roots and into the seabed?
>
> We recommend that you consider these questions well before you choose the anchor you will use in weeds, or in any other bottom, if the design you plan to use will not readily set on its own.

since weeds and their roots do not provide as good of holding for an anchor as does the seabed in which they are growing. Thus, in this type of growth, more often than not, getting most anchors to set and hold can range from not-likely to non-existent.

For an anchor to obtain the best holding it must be heavy enough to crush down to the bottom and have arms or flukes long enough to penetrate below the roots into the seabed itself. In reality, few anchors can do this. In fact, it is our opinion that the only one that can do this reliably is the fisherman-style anchor.

Other than a fisherman-style anchor, anchors that manage to set in weeds usually just hook into the weeds or their roots, and some anchors cannot do even this. Instead, they just lie on top of the weeds, with the boat ground-tied. As a result, the mariner who anchors in weeds is often "anchored" with a false sense of security, and is usually caught off guard when the wind pipes up and his anchor pulls out or drags. Then, he is faced with the additional problem of getting the anchor, probably clogged, to reset in the same bottom it just pulled out of. In weeds, if the anchor trips or drags, checking to see if it needs cleared is mandatory before trying to reset it.

With designs other than a fisherman-style anchor, the best rule is to use them only where weed growth is sparse; any anchor that cannot set any deeper than the roots should, in weeds, be considered a fair weather anchor only. So, as the wind rises, the captain has two choices: either deploy an anchor better suited to this type bottom or move the boat elsewhere.

To our way of looking at this, it's better to have onboard and use an anchor that can dig in below the roots to set into the bottom in which the weeds are growing, and is also big enough to resist the highest winds that will be encountered.

Size the anchor as in Chapter 6 for the type of bottom in which the weeds are growing.

ROCK

A "rock" bottom, not to be confused with a "rocky" bottom, is a continuous, essentially unbroken expanse of rock or coral which may or may not be covered with a too-thin layer of soil. Bottoms like this pose a unique challenge in that the only way to secure a boat to a "rock" seabed is to auger in an anchor, or use brute weight.

An anchor will catch and release, or just skip along the top of a rock bottom, but on occasion, it may hook into a crack or crevice. When the rock bottom is covered with a thin layer of soil, the anchor might dig in, but just enough to give a false sense of security. Either situation, is at best tenuous, for with a rising wind, especially when coupled with a shift in either the wind or current, the anchor is likely to drag or trip. Even multiple anchors, since no one anchor will be able to get a strong enough grip in bottoms like this, will most likely be unsuccessful if the wind speed rises.

One technique that you can use with a bottom like this is to drop the anchor, then, to avoid fouling it, back off 50 feet or so and dump 200+ feet of chain in one pile. As the chain pulls out, the friction of the chain on the bottom develops some holding power, adding to the holding power of the remaining weight of the pile of chain.

Tandem anchors is another approach that can be used, placing more weight on the bottom, plus the additional anchor and rode creates more boat-holding friction. When the bottom is covered with a thin layer of soil, if one or both anchors can bull-doze up a hump of soil ahead of it, all the better.

With this in mind, one unconventional way of using this technique would be to deploy fisherman anchors or Northill anchors without their stocks. With this arrangement, the anchors, lying flat, have more surface area in contact with the bottom, not only providing for more friction-holding capacity, but for a bigger "hump" of soil bull-dozed up in front of them.

The problem with these techniques is, as the wind rises, it's hard to know at what point they lose their effectiveness, requiring that you abandon this approach and seek better arrangements, and as is typical in anchoring, it is better to do so too early, rather than too late.

CARRY MORE THAN ONE ANCHOR

To offset the possibility that the boat will be anchored in an area where the anchor will not perform well, one common suggestion is to carry more than one type of anchor, so "if one anchor does not work, maybe the other will". While this is good advice, it's another somewhat misleading statement. Rather than just carrying two different types of anchors, hoping that one will work, those anchors that you do choose should be of a specific design, weight, and size that will excel in the type of bottom in which they will be used. This is a subtle, but important distinction.

SHACKLE SLOTS

Some anchors have a slot along the length of the shank in which the shackle is installed. Placing the shackle in this slot carries with it the risk that, with a shift of wind or current, the shackle can slide back along the shank, allowing the anchor to be pulled out backwards.

If this function of the design is not desired, and the anchor manufacturer does not provide a device that inserts into the slot to prevent this backward sliding of the shackle, one can easily be made using fender washers or similar items, placed one on each side of the slot, and held together with a bolt and nut, or the slot can be strongly moused.

DESIGNS

FISHERMAN-STYLE ANCHORS

Classic, Admiralty Pattern, Old-Fashion, Traditional, Yachtsman, Luke, Herreshoff, Kingston, and other like styles. When it comes to setting

 and holding in a wide variety of bottoms, these anchors are probably the best all-round anchors on the market. As such, it is an especially good anchor to carry onboard when a variety of unknown types of bottoms, especially weeds, will be encountered. Because of this ability, it is our opinion that the fisherman-style anchor can be the ultimate fallback, fail-safe anchor, particularly when another anchor's performance may be questionable.

For general use, traditionally-dimensioned designs with moderate-size palms are best; the Luke and Kingston models are good examples. For exceptionally soft bottoms, if a large fluke design is not available, a bigger anchor can be substituted. Another possibility is to weld additional material onto the palms of the existing anchor. Models with narrow palms are useful in coral. For hard bottoms, the palms should be sharpened, maybe ground down some in width, or possibly you can locate a narrower-palm design.

This anchor is occasionally thought to perform poorly in sand or mud, but our experiences, as well as others, suggest otherwise. We suspect that any failures of this anchor in these bottoms usually result from:

- The anchor being undersized for the conditions;
- The anchor was not built to traditional-dimension; or
- Inadequate scope was involved.

As with all anchors, the fisherman anchor has a few idiosyncrasies. One is the "lazy arm," the arm that sticks up out of the bottom, on which the rode can foul. As with any anchor, if the wind is expected to clock around or the current shift, it is prudent to set out an additional anchor or two, and more so if the risk of rode wrap exists (see Appendix 7).

With its arms and stock oriented perpendicular to one another and situated at opposite ends of the anchor's shank, this anchor requires special arrangements to be deployed, retrieved, or stowed. On the other hand, if the anchor is a take-apart design, such as the Luke and Kingston designs, it will be easier to stow, or to manhandle around the boat, in the dinghy, or onshore as the manhandling can be done piece-by-piece.

Also, with take-apart models, a second hole, if not already present, can be drilled in the shank so that the shackle and stock can be installed or removed independently of one another. When doing so, be certain that the two holes are spaced far enough apart so that the eye of the shackle and the stop on the stock do not interfere with each other. Models are also available where the stock folds down to house along the shank. With a folding or removable stock, these anchors are convenient to stow on deck.

Since anchors sized for long-duration, storm-force conditions are rarely carried in a bow roller, should anchoring in such conditions be necessary, outfitting with a take apart fisherman-style anchor(s) makes an excellent, and often better alternative to outfitting with more contemporary anchor designs.

Another issue with this design is devising a suitable way to get this often heavy, and usually awkward-to-handle anchor on and off the boat. We use a boom, along with tackle, but on other boats a davit or cat-head makes the job less onerous; with some ingenuity, no doubt there are other arrangements that will work.

> **TIP:** Do not forget to also make suitable arrangements to the dinghy for the possibility of using it for getting any anchor out or back aboard.

This anchor is so effective in so many types of bottoms that the effort to make these arrangements will be well worth the time and effort to do so.

NORTHILL STYLE ANCHORS

These anchors are excellent in sand, mud, clay, marl, rocks, and depending on their size and spacing, boulders. To offset the limiting effect the stock has on this anchor's ability to bury deeply, while still enabling this anchor to develop good holding, this anchor is usually made with large palms. A Northill anchor that's heavy enough and has large palms can set in weeds, but there is a risk that it can pull out in rising winds if the palms do not extend below the roots into the seabed.

With this design, the stock and its very short arms with their attached palms are both located at the anchor's crown. That makes the Northill anchor easy to house in a roller, though difficult to stow on deck. For deck stowage, this inconvenience can be remedied by choosing one of the models which has a stock that can be withdrawn or folded down. Take-apart designs are also available.

The palms on a Northill anchor can be sized specific to the type of bottom in which the anchor will be used simply by adding to or cutting away material from the existing palms.

This anchor, too, has a "lazy arm" that often sticks up out of the seabed. As with any anchor on which the rode can foul, this liability is countered by setting out more than one anchor (see Appendix 7).

In commercial fishing areas, Northill-style anchors are usually made by local welders or machine shops. If you're a good welder there is no reason you can't do the same by simply copying an existing anchor.

The Pekny anchor, a lightweight, usually folding, Northill design, comes with different sizes of palms, interchangeable for various types of seabeds. But, having insufficient weight to drive its palms into a hard bottom, the Pekny anchor can be expected to perform poorly in this type of bottom unless a palm happens to grab a crevice, crack, or hole.

STOCK-STABILIZED, PIVOTING-FLUKE ANCHORS

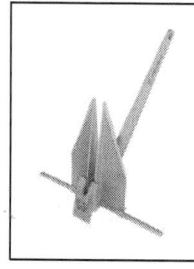

Danforth, Fortress, Guardian, U.S. Navy Mark II LWT, and similar style anchors, work well in sand, mud, small rocks, and depending on their spacing, boulders. Because of their high holding-power-to-weight ratio, in compatible bottoms, these designs, whether steel or aluminum, is a practical choice as a second anchor or kedge anchor.

In soft bottoms, in particular, the aluminum models of this style, even with mud palms installed, often bury their shanks first, which interferes with the ability of the flukes to dig in. To minimize this tendency, your best approach when setting these anchors using a "short" scope–3:1, maybe 2:1–which tends to keep the shank "up", which encourages the flukes to dig in. Once the flukes begin to dig in, a longer rode can be used while further setting the anchor.

In weeds, big steel Danforth-style anchors usually grab on, but they only dig into the weeds, maybe the roots, not the seabed itself, and that makes them susceptible to pulling out once the wind speed rises or with a shift in direction of the wind or current. Once they pull out, they are usually clogged; this mandates that they first be cleared before any attempt to reset them occurs.

During the seven months that we studied anchor behavior, not one Fortress anchor that we observed, regardless of size, would set in weeds. This finding is not only frequently reported by other mariners, but the manufacturer also cautions against using this anchor in weeds.

Unless stock-stabilized, pivoting fluke anchors set deep, which usually does not occur in hard, or even firm bottoms, especially if the vessel is low-powered, a shift in wind or current often cause these designs to trip, and if tripped, prior to being reset, the anchor must be checked to see if it is fouled. In situations like this, setting multiple anchors should be considered mandatory (see Appendix 7).

Fortress FX series, as well as a few other more obscure stock-stabilized, pivoting-fluke designs, have flukes that are adjustable to either 32 or 45-degrees. With these anchors, for sand, clay, rocks, firm mud and marl, the fluke angle should be set at the shallow 32-degree setting, but for the most effectiveness in soft mud, the fluke angle should be adjusted to the deeper 45-degree setting. However, even with the fluke angle set at 45-degrees, the anchor may still need to be bigger to have the amount of holding power that the boat requires. If the bigger anchor does not have a 45-degree fluke angle, it may have to be even bigger for the necessary holding power.

Some of these models, such as the Fortress FX, Guardian, and some Mark II anchors, can be taken apart, which helps with the chore of stowage. This also allows you to carry a much bigger anchor, since it can be manhandled around piece by piece, and if sized appropriately and used in a compatible bottom, this type of anchor makes a good storm anchor. However, since squalls, gales, and storms are usually accompanied with shifting winds, setting multiple anchors when using this type of anchor as a main bower would be wise in order to eliminate the risk of the anchor tripping

These style anchors are prone to bent shanks, flukes, or stocks when heavy strains are encountered, a situation that often occurs in order to get them to release from the bottom, particularly if they are deeply buried.

NAVY STOCKLESS STYLE ANCHORS

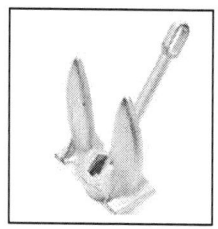

Navy, Babbit, Hall, Pol, Stato, and other similar style anchors are designed with a 45-degree fluke angle for use in mud, though they are also useful in rocks, and depending on their spacing, boulders. These anchors are seldom large enough to encircle boulders of any size, and due to blunt flukes, they perform poorly in hard and firm bottoms. Due to the 45-degree fluke angle, we consider them a poor choice for use in sand, clay, firm mud, or marl. These designs very seldom set to any significant depth in weeds, even when the weeds are growing in mud; when they do, the anchor is subject to the idiosyncrasies noted in the WEEDS section above.

Unless they are of a very large size, relative to the size of the boat, we don't believe that these anchors should be relied upon in rising winds, even in mud. Author Earl Hinz states, in *The Complete Book of Anchoring and Mooring*, that in mud the holding power of this style of anchor is generally accepted to be no more than 3X its weight.

In spite of their limitations, what makes these designs popular with larger vessels is the ease with which they can be stowed in hawse pipes. If these anchors fail to bury deeply, they have a tendency to trip when side-loaded, thus, if shifting winds or currents are expected these designs would benefit from having additional anchors deployed (see Appendix 7).

DELTA and SIMILAR *FIXED*-SHANK PLOW ANCHORS

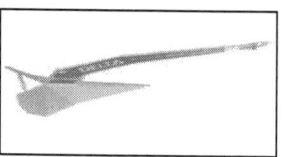

Delta anchors and others like them are good in sand, mud, rocks, clay, marl, rocks, and depending on their size and spacing, boulders. Our observations of these designs reveal that they very seldom set in weeds, and when they do, the anchor is subject to the idiosyncrasies noted in the WEEDS section above.

CQR and SIMILAR HINGED-SHANK PLOW ANCHORS

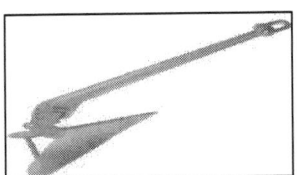 These style anchors are generally good in sand, mud, rocks, and depending on their size and spacing, boulders. With the hinge, this style anchor, the thinking goes, when lying on a hard or firm bottom, causes the shank, relative to the flukes, to be pushed up, altering the angle that the flukes need in order to dig into the seabed. This inhibits the anchor's ability to set. Due to this idiosyncrasy, in hard, firm, or other difficult-to-set-in-bottoms, setting with a "long" scope, in an attempt to keep the shank down, might help them set.

Once set, the hinge in the shank assists in the anchor's ability to remain set during wind and current shifts. But, when the angle of pull reaches the maximum point of the hinge's travel, these hinged-shank anchors have a tendency to trip, therefore, in conditions like this, the use of multiple anchors should be considered (see Appendix 7).

During our seven month observation of anchor behavior, in weeds this design had a low percentage of setting. When it did, it was subject to the idiosyncrasies noted in the WEEDS section above.

BRUCE and SIMILAR CLAW ANCHORS

Bruce and other claw anchors are generally good in sand, mud, clay, marl, rocks, and depending on size and spacing, boulders.

During our observation of anchors in weedy anchorages, we noted that this anchor sets in weeds less frequently than plow anchors, and when it did set, it was subject to the idiosyncrasies noted in the WEEDS section above.

This design is awkward to stow on deck, but it stows well in a roller of compatible design. There is anecdotal evidence that suggests that "copy-cat" claw anchors suffer performance problems that the original Bruce anchor does not have. Unfortunately, the original Bruce anchor is no longer in production, but used Bruce anchors can occasionally be had.

Super MAX ANCHOR

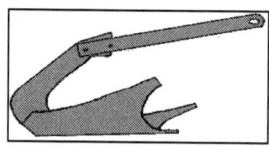

This is a three-toed, "scoop" anchor with a three-position, adjustable shank that is excellent in sand, mud, clay, marl, rocks, and depending on their size and spacing, boulders. It is also available in a rigid, non-adjustable shank model.

The anchor's creator claims that this anchor sets in weeds, but our experience shows that not to be the case unless the weed growth is rather sparse. Others have indicated that their experiences with this anchor mirror ours, so, in our opinion, this anchor is subject to the same idiosyncrasies noted in the WEEDS section above.

If you are going to use an adjustable model in a bottom where the sparsity of the weed growth is compatible with allowing this anchor to set, the fluke angle needs to be adjusted for the type of bottom in which the weeds are growing.

Although the Super MAX anchor was not included in the 2014 Chesapeake Bay Test, we, and others have found that this anchor sets easily in mud, regardless of how it is deployed. In spite of this observation, proper technique in deploying and setting this anchor should still be observed.

The features of the Super MAX anchor–its good weight distribution, and three "thin", strong, sharp-edged toes, along with the fluke's angle of attack–allows for the anchor's ease of setting. With high-tensile steel for strength, and large fluke area, this anchor has the ability to develop extremely high holding power.

Though not the most attractive anchor on the market, with its ability to set in so many types of bottoms, and its propensity to remain set in shifting winds or changing currents, added into its other list of advantages, it is our opinion that the Super MAX anchor out-performs any other contemporary anchors we have used, experimented with, or observed in action.

Although we would like to claim that the Fisherman anchor is the best general, all-round anchor on the market, its awkwardness in handling and stowage makes it second on our list, with first place going to the Super MAX anchor.

SPADE and SIMILAR *NON*-ROLL BAR SCOOP ANCHORS

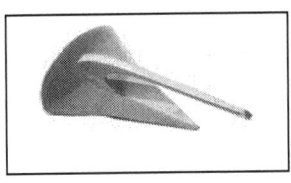

The Spade and other *non*-roll bar scoop anchors perform well in sand, mud, clay, marl, rocks, and depending on their size and spacing, boulders. They are subject to the idiosyncrasies noted in the WEEDS section above.

In the 2014 Chesapeake Bay anchor test, the "Spade" anchor, was an exception to the other designs tested. Although it was just average in holding power, in spite of having been subjected to poor deployment technique, it never just dragged along the mud bottom without setting. The testers hypothesized that this was due to its high concentration of weight in its tip, causing it to orient itself correctly enough to set.

The "Spade" anchor has a removable shank, easing the problems of finding stowage, or for carrying it around the boat, on shore, or in the dinghy.

ROLL-BAR SCOOP ANCHORS

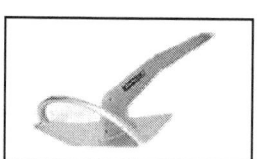

Rocna, Mantus, Manson Supreme and other similar style anchors are good in sand, mud, clay, marl, rocks, and depending on their size and spacing, boulders. In soft bottoms, as mentioned in the MUD section, these anchors are reliant on good deployment technique. The manufacturer claims good setting in weeds, but our observations strongly suggest that these designs are subject to all of the idiosyncrasies noted in the WEEDS section above.

SPECIALTY ANCHORS

The coral pick, mushroom, grapnel, and sea anchor designs comprise the bulk of this category, with each design created for a particular type of bottom or for a specific use. None are considered all-around general purpose anchors, nor should they be treated as such. We do not cover them in this book.

ANCHORING IN MUD

Until the anchor digs deep enough to encounter enough resistance, it just pulls through the bottom, or if the load is high enough, it can pull right out. This is true for all bottoms, but it seems to occur more readily in mud. During the 2014 test of a dozen anchors of varying designs conducted by Fortress Marine Anchors in the mud of Chesapeake Bay, not one of the 12 anchors tested, regardless of design, showed significant resistance in the mud until it reached sufficient depth, which typically required pulling the anchor at least 30-40 feet through the bottom. In a few of the pulls, even greater distances were required. And of the anchors that did dig in, it was determined, either by direct measurement or by back-calculating, that some of these anchors had buried at least 10 feet into the mud, and a few were suspected of burying even deeper.

One important lesson that we learned from this test is that this 30, 40, or more feet must be allowed for when setting anchors in mud, in addition to having enough swing room for the boat once enough rode has been deployed. A corollary to this issue is that, if the anchor trips, it will again require this 30, 40, or more feet to reset, if it will reset at all.

TWO OTHER OPTIONS

So that's what you can expect when setting an anchor in soft bottoms using the "standard approach". But you can often set anchors in much shorter distances using one of these techniques:

- Pull and Pause (aka: Tugging) - The anchor is deployed and a load is applied, very lightly at first. Then the load on the anchor is eased and all active setting of the anchor is paused for a moment. The "pull and pause" approach is repeated with the load on the anchor slowly increasing during each pull. This demands that the helmsman be alert for any feel that, instead of settling in deeper, the anchor is pulling out, or is just pulling through the bottom. If the helmsman senses that the anchor is at the point where it will pull out or is just pulling through the bottom, the load on the anchor should be removed. Then, after a pause, light power is applied and the process resumed. This technique could also be of benefit when you are trying to get an anchor to set in hard, firm, or other bottoms, when setting the anchor is difficult.

- Deploy and Delay (aka: Soaking) - The anchor is deployed but left to sit with no significant load, depending on the "softness" of the bottom, for 15-30 minutes or more, allowing the anchor to sink into the mud before any attempt is made to set it. When it's time to pull back on the anchor, light and slow is the rule. Good senses and a deft feel by the helmsman will help assure that the load on the anchor does not exceed the point where the anchor pulls out of the bottom or through it. If the anchor begins to pull through the bottom or pulls out, the load should be removed, and the anchor should again be allowed to "soak" awhile before a load is again applied.

EMERGENCY-BRAKING ANCHOR

This is one anchor that must set immediately, every time that it is deployed. In an emergency-braking anchor, weight is a decided advantage, as is having a design that is suited to easily setting in the type of bottom in which it will be used. It must also be large enough and strong enough, that once it sets, to be able to resist the load developed from the momentum of the moving boat.

To avoid shock loading when the boat fetches up hard after the anchor sets, Nylon rope, one of large diameter, would be the rode of choice for this type of anchoring (see Chapter 5). To facilitate setting, especially if the boat has way on, a copious length of rode may need to first be deployed.

If a chain rode will be employed, have a shock-absorbing length of Nylon line on the chain's bitter end; make it of large diameter and 30 feet or more in length. If damage to the windlass is a possibility, do not brake the windlass, let all of the chain, plus the 30 feet of line go out. This necessitates that the end of the line is attached to the boat, and that enough distance is available to allow all of the rode to go out. If the needed room will be lacking, use an all Nylon rode.

Since the load on an emergency stopping anchor can be, depending on the speed and size of the boat, anywhere from significant to huge, any snubbing and belaying point(s) must be extremely strong, both in design and in their attachment to the boat.

ONE SPECIAL BIG ANCHOR

Having that one anchor, one that is big enough and can set in just about any type of bottom has the advantage that it can be deployed anytime, essentially guaranteeing that the boat will stay put, no "ifs, ands or buts", regardless of the circumstances. This provides for that proverbial peace-of-mind, something that cannot be gotten any other way. For this purpose, since it can be used in just about any type of bottom, and most importantly in weeds, we favor carrying a large-enough, traditional-dimensioned Fisherman anchor, set up so it can be deployed quickly.

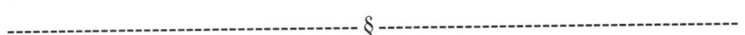

Remember that schooner we mentioned at the beginning of this chapter? Did you wonder whether it ended up in the shoals? Well, it came close, but fortunately, it did not.

When it dragged we were not surprised. After all, the anchors the captain decided to use were two of the many anchors that, based on our observations, perform poorly in that bottom of dense weeds. And there was the issue of the boat only being "ground-tied".

After a lot of yelling and frantic effort, the crew managed to recover their anchors. And, yep, you guessed it, it was their big, old-fashion fisherman anchor that they then put to work. That fisherman anchor set immediately, even though it was set in the exact same spot where they first anchored. At that point, the yelling ceased, and that schooner sat peacefully the remainder of the night, not budging an inch.

EXAMPLES - CHAPTER 7

Here is the inventory of the ground tackle for the authors' boat, a 34' LOA x 12' beam x 4'9" draft, 25,000 lb., full displacement, long keeled, raised-sheer, sail-assisted trawler. This gear has proven more than adequate through long-duration, 60-knot winds, in soft mud, even where the protection from seas was poor. This same gear has been used successfully, multiple times, in Category I, II and III hurricane force winds with the boat anchored where the protection from seas was moderate to good.

- 50-lb. Super MAX (adjustable) anchor- This is our main bower, housed on an anchor platform, attached to 250 feet of 5/16 inch High Test Chain. Its bitter end is attached to a 30-foot, 5/8 inch diameter, 3-strand, Nylon pendant, whose bitter end is secured within the rode locker.

- 70 lb. Luke anchor- This is a three-piece, take-apart fisherman-style anchor and is our primary storm anchor. It is the only anchor that we depend on in weeds. It is also the anchor that gets deployed anytime that we are uncomfortable with lying only to our main bower. It can also be deployed as a second anchor or switched to be our main bower should the Super MAX anchor be slipped or lost. This anchor is kept assembled, chocked-down on the foredeck with its stock folded; it is retrieved by the use of a boom, outfitted with tackle. To deploy this anchor with two people, it is simply "one, two, three", and tossed overboard, brought back up to be cleared, if fouled, then lowered and set. With one person, deployment is with the boom, the anchor temporarily belayed to the bottom block with a slipped knot. Once the anchor is over the water, the knot is slipped, freeing the anchor to drop. This anchor's rode is coiled and kept on deck. For rough weather this rode is securely lashed to the anchor, but otherwise always ready for immediate deployment.

- 100 lb. Luke anchor- This, too, is a three-piece, take-apart fisherman-style anchor, which is our hurricane anchor. We also use it in weeds when we need to deploy a second anchor and diving on an anchor is not practical or possible. This anchor is stowed disassembled, securely tied down in the bilge. This anchor is deployed and retrieved only with the use of the boom and tackle as mentioned in the paragraph above.

- Fortress FX-16 anchor- This is an aluminum, adjustable, stock-stabilized, pivoting-fluke anchor, used as a second anchor or as a kedge anchor. It is small enough that it can function as an anchor for our dinghy. It is stowed, chocked upright in place on the engine room door.

- Fortress FX-37 anchor- This is an aluminum, adjustable, stock-stabilized, pivoting fluke anchor used primarily as a second anchor or as a kedge anchor should we need more holding power than the FX-16 can provide. This anchor is stowed positioned up-right against and lashed to one of the pilot house roof supports.

- 5 lb. folding grapnel anchor- This is our primary dinghy anchor, kept stowed in a canvas bag that is attached under the seat of the dinghy. Its rode is 3/8 inch, 3-strand Nylon, and for convenience is made up into two coils, one shorter than the other. When the full length is required, these two coils are bent together.

- 3 lb. Danforth anchor- This is a secondary dinghy anchor to be used whenever the grappling hook anchor will not be adequate. It is stowed in the bilge of the trawler, and a similar rode as is used for the grapnel anchor is used with this anchor.

- Rodes- We have one complete rode for each anchor. As mentioned, our main bower is all chain secured to the boat with a 3-strand nylon pendant. The remainder of the rodes are all rope (3-strand, 8-plait, or 12-braid). These rope rodes vary in size from ¾ inch to 1 3/16 inch in diameter. As we cruise in areas with plenty of "shallow" anchorages, each rode is a minimum of 200 feet in length. We also carry a few short sections of 5/16 inch and 3/8 inch High Test chain that can be interchanged among the various rodes and anchors. All sections of chain have oversized links in their ends. It is not unusual for us to carry an additional 200-400 feet of 1 inch line. These lines are coiled, lashed with "small stuff" and stowed in the bilge.

- Snubbers- We carry a variety–3/4" x 40', 7/8" x 40', and 1 3/16" x 40', all 3-strand nylon rope. Each have "snubber braids" put in their ends and are attached to the rodes using a rolling hitch (see Chapter 5).

- Six- 7/8 inch x 30-40 foot "dock" lines.

- Several- 1/2 or 5/8 inch x 30-50 foot "docking" lines.

- Assorted sizes of regular strength (carbon) shackles and high strength (alloy) shackles, 5/8 inch and 3/4 inch swivels, 3/4 x 6 inch rings, skeins of "small stuff", whipping twine, and leather anti-chafe gear.

- 100 feet each- 1/4 inch, 3/8 inch, and 1/2 inch 3-strand Nylon or polyester rope.

- ABI horizontal manual windlass- 3/8" gypsy which works well with our 5/16" NACM G4 chain, and with 3/4 inch or 7/8 inch 3-strand or 8-plait rope.

- Time and again we have found that the ability to splice any of the types of rope onboard to be an extremely useful skill to possess.

CHAPTER 8

SCOPE

As we entered the small Bahamian cove, we could see that anchoring here was going to be tight. Shortly after we got our anchors set, a forty-something foot sloop entered, squeezing in to anchor upwind of us. With this neighbor on a suspiciously short scope and the wind forecast to reach close to gale force level, our concern was raised. But since the wind was also predicted to clock around, swinging him away from us, we decided to wait and see.

Sure enough, as the wind clocked around our neighbor swung away from us, and as the wind speed increased the boat began to drag. Fortunately someone was on the boat. But after watching for a few minutes it became obvious that he was alone and was having difficulty retrieving both of his anchors, while at the same time trying to keep his boat out of the shallows. So we dinghied over and our offer to help was met with an enthusiastic "yes".

As we helped him retrieve his ground tackle, our suspicions were confirmed; his main bower had only about 50-60 feet of rode, while his second anchor had somewhat less. After getting the boat re-anchored, this pleasant, young skipper expressed surprise that his anchors had dragged. He thought that since he was in 10 feet of water, the 60 feet of rode would be enough, particularly since one rode was all chain. "After all", he said, "isn't that what the books suggest—all chain, use 5:1 scope, right?" Well... let's see!

118

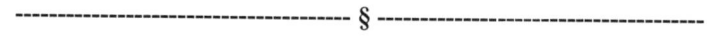

Scope is "the ratio of the length of line in use to the distance to the bottom of the water as measured from the deck."
Chapman- Piloting, Seamanship and Small Boat Handling

The principle behind scope is simple: as the rode's pull on the anchor becomes more vertical, the easier it is for the anchor to pull out of the bottom. After all, this is the principle used when weighing anchor. It is also the cause of many boats dragging.

On the other hand, the smaller the angle between the rode and the bottom, the "rode-to-bottom angle", the better the anchor will hold. One of the easiest and most practical ways to make the rode-to-bottom angle smaller is to pay out more rode, moving the boat farther away from the anchor, the farther the better. But how far is "far enough"?

RULES-OF-THUMB

The long-used rules-of-thumb for calculating scope–10:1 for rope, 7:1 for half rope/half chain, and 5:1 for all-chain–work because some of the rode's catenary, the sag in the rode due to its own weight, is lying on the seabed allowing a rode-to-bottom angle of zero. It also creates some boat-holding friction with the seabed. It just doesn't get any better than this. But the problem, and it is often a big problem, is that these rules-of-thumb apply only in mild weather.

BETTER OPTION

As the wind picks up the rode straightens, decreasing the catenary. This is where the danger lies... once the rode begins to lift off of the bottom, the anchor's holding power starts to decrease. In addition, as the rode lifts off of the bottom the boat-holding friction that comes from the rode lying on the bottom is lost, further reducing the ground tackle's holding power.

When you are thinking about how scope affects an anchor's holding ability, consider this:

- The makers of Fortress anchors indicate that a 10:1 scope gives an anchor twice the holding power of a 5:1 scope. For a more eye-opening look, let's turn that around: an anchor with scope of 5:1 has only half the holding power as the same anchor with 10:1 scope.

- Other research, which we believe was conducted by Alan Hylas, also addresses this subject: a scope of 4:1 elicits only 55 percent of the anchor's maximum holding power, while 10:1 elicits 85 percent. One hundred percent holding power requires the rode lying horizontally on the bottom.

Then there is the issue of the rode-to-bottom angle. The importance of the rode-to-bottom angle is underscored by a British Royal Navy test showing that when an anchor's stock, compared to the bottom (what we call the rode-to-bottom angle) had an angle of 10 degrees, the anchor lost 40 percent of its holding power; and at 15 degrees, the loss was 60 percent (Admiralty Manual of Seamanship, Vol. 2).

For these figures to make sense in a useful way, we need to convert rode-to-bottom angles to scope. In a rode without essentially any contributing catenary, 10:1 scope produces a 6 degree rode-to-bottom angle; 7:1 scope produces around a 9 degree rode-to-bottom angle; while 5:1 scope produces around a 12 degree rode-to-bottom angle.

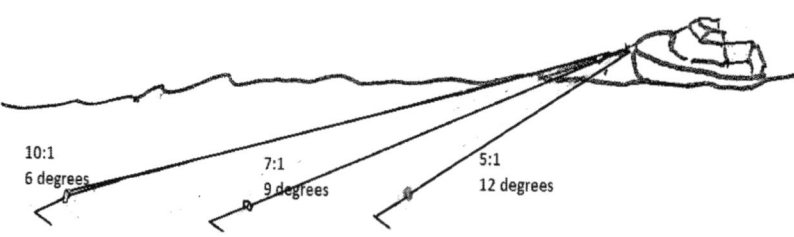

10:1
6 degrees

7:1
9 degrees

5:1
12 degrees

> *No matter how it is stated, the message should be clear:*
> *As the wind speed increases, the long-used "rules-of-thumb" for*
> *scope, since they become less and less effective, need to be discarded.*
> *The focus should, instead, be directed toward achieving and*
> *maintaining a low rode-to-bottom angle, an angle that does not*
> *exceed 6 degrees.*

DISAPPEARING CATENARY

We once read that an "old timer" said, "at 40 knots, there ain't no catenary". Yes, this is true... when the rode is all chain; but, should the rode be part or all rope, or if the boat is anchored where the protection from seas is "poor", then the catenary will disappear sooner.

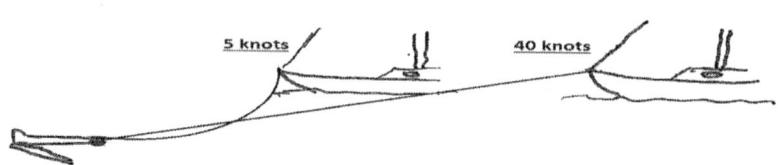

5 knots   40 knots

Does this mean that every boat should be outfitted with a wind speed instrument, and when anchored, the crew should keep their eyes glued to it? Probably not, as a simpler, but yet eminently practical approach is available... just take a walk forward and peek at the rode.

If the rode looks like it is beginning to straighten out, which it will start to do as the wind speed exceeds 15-20 knots, then the focus should switch to getting and maintaining a low rode-to-bottom angle. So the stronger the wind, the longer the rode should be. Once the catenary has essentially disappeared, the boat, to maintain this 6 degree rode-to-bottom angle, should be lying to a scope of 10:1. Keep in mind that the catenary will disappear at wind speeds lower than 40 knots if the rode is fiber rope or if the boat is anchored where the protection from seas is poor.

BEING PROACTIVE

There is no question that when higher winds are forecast, plenty of scope should be let out. But what about those times when the rode cannot be let out in a timely manner?

Sometimes high winds can hit so quickly that there is no chance to let out more rode before the anchor is at risk of dragging. Sudden squalls or one of those hard-to-see-coming nighttime thunder(less) storms, especially if the crew is asleep or off the boat, are two great examples.

If high winds are possible, no matter how short lived that they may be, it's best to be preemptive by making certain you have out enough scope. This usually equates to a scope of 10:1 (6 degree rode-to-bottom angle). Then, as long as the strength of all the gear is adequate, the anchor's size and design are appropriate for the bottom, good anti-chafe techniques are employed, along with the possible need for the use of multiple anchors, the ground tackle should be able to handle, without assistance, these high, but usually short-lived winds.

MORE IS BETTER THAN LESS

In *The Complete Book of Anchoring and Mooring*, Earl Hinz writes, "In general, anchors for small boats are designed for a lead angle–what we are calling the rode-to-bottom angle–of not more than 8 degrees (7:1 scope), and the user should see to it that the lead angle is much less so that the anchor flukes can dig in with a will". This latter part, "... and the user should see to it that the lead angle is much less... ", we fully support, as we have seen too many boats drag when using a 7:1 scope, a situation that is often resolved if the rode is then let out to achieve a scope of 10:1. When the full holding power of the anchor is required, this anecdotal evidence presents a strong argument for relying on 10:1 scope, not 7:1.

CALCULATING SCOPE

Typically, scope is calculated by adding all of the following together:

- The depth of the water where the anchor is set;
- The height from the water surface to the deck, bow roller, hawse hole, or chock; and,
- Any additional height contributed by the tide.

BUT... IN ROUGH WEATHER

When the wind rises, the cause for anchors that drag or trip is often attributed to surge loads, but we have a strong suspicion that many of these incidents are caused by too little scope, the crew having failed to take into account three additional critical factors: 1) storm surge; 2) height of waves; and, 3) the anchor's depth of bury.

STORM SURGE

During storms, gales, and even during periods where the wind remains steady from one direction for a period of time, the depth of water

123

can increase beyond normal heights. An easy to remember, though rough guide for estimating the height of storm surge is based on a factor of 3: gales and storms, 1-3 feet; Category I hurricane, 3 feet; Category II hurricane, 6 feet; Category III hurricane, 9 feet; Category IV hurricane, 12 feet; Category V hurricane, 15 feet.

Storm surges can be even higher, especially under the following conditions: the longer the wind blows; the lower the barometric pressure; the closer the moon is to full, new, or perigee; during summer; when there is no geographic interference to the flow of water; or where they occur, during seiches.

WAVES

As the boat crests a wave, the depth of water under the boat increases, and this additional height will cause the rode-to-bottom angle to increase. Waves can range in height from almost nothing in well protected anchorages, to 6 feet or more in exposed anchorages.

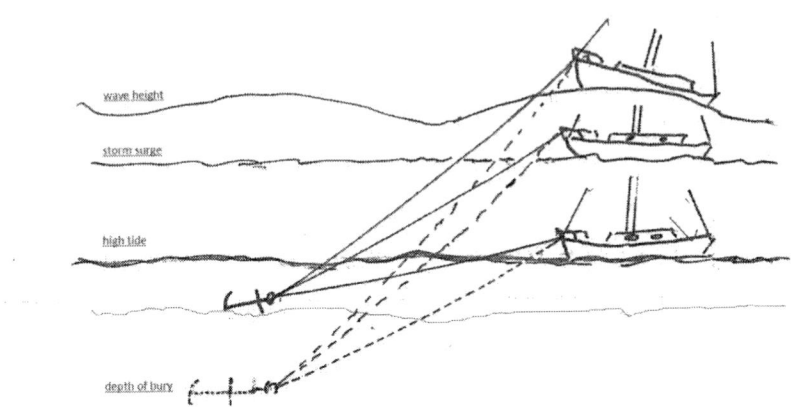

DEPTH OF BURY

In soft bottoms the anchor will bury deeper than in firmer bottoms, and in severe conditions, often to a considerable depth. We've had experiences where our anchor has buried many feet, and one boater told us that his anchor, in a "mucky" bottom, buried at least 8 feet. During a comparison test of 12 different anchors in 2014, sponsored by Fortress Anchors, there were instances of anchors burying 10 feet with loads that would equate to wind speeds close to gale force level.

> **NOT ENOUGH ROOM?**
> If you have inadequate room to lie to one long-enough rode, deploying additional anchors, all with adequate scope, but positioned to limit the amount of room that the boat requires to swing, may resolve the issue (see Appendix 7). If that doesn't work, instead of risking lying to less scope, you may need to find a different place to anchor.

Trying to determine, ahead of time, exactly how deep the anchor will bury is often a futile exercise, so the best rule to follow is simple: when in doubt, assume that more scope is needed, not less.

Fail to take into account all six of these factors—depth of water, the boat's freeboard, additional tide, storm surge, wave height, and depth of bury—when calculating scope, and the chances are that the length of rode paid out will end up woefully too short.

SCOPE GREATER THAN 10:1

We have often seen it written that using scope greater than 10:1 changes the rode-to-bottom angle so slightly, it's a waste of time. As far as geometry is concerned, that is correct; but there is more to scope than geometry... there is reality.

As the conditions become more severe, using scope greater than 10:1 may provide some tolerance against any errors that might have creeped in when calculating for the length of rode needed, even though, after-the-fact, it may be impossible to prove that this additional length was necessary.

But, if the height of the storm surge, height of the waves, and the depth of the anchor's bury, among the other factors that need to be included in the calculations were either underestimated or omitted, then a scope of greater than 10:1 should be considered mandatory.

SCOPE FOR SETTING vs SCOPE FOR HOLDING

Although anchors have better holding power if a longer rode is employed, the amount of rode that will allow some anchors to set is often much less. If the anchor being used might trip and cannot reset while on long scope, then about the only option available to avoid this conundrum is to deploy multiple anchors in a pattern such that one anchor, in concert with the other(s), will prevent any one anchor from tripping (see Appendix 7). Thus, with the risk of tripping removed, each anchor can be set with an eye toward having enough scope to ensure good holding.

BIGGER ANCHORS vs LESS SCOPE

We recommended earlier, that with "The Big 5"–anchor size, anchor design, strength, scope, and anti-chafe techniques–no one of these be substituted to do the job of another due to the attendant increase in risk that the anchor will trip, drag, or that the boat will break free. While this is true, there is one exception, and that is when the anchor's holding power is great enough to offset the holding power lost due to use of shorter scope.

> **MORE SCOPE vs INADEQUATE ANCHORS**
>
> When the anchor drags, and time and space allow, the first option could be to pay out more rode. However, deploying more rode to counter an anchor that is too small to begin with, is of the wrong design for the bottom, or has fouled, has its limits. With any of these situations, the problem with dragging will not likely be resolved until the problem with the anchor is first resolved.

Theoretically, if this trade-off is made, the anchor will not drag or trip, but:

- The load on the ground tackle must not be underestimated;

- The holding power of the anchor must not be overestimated;
- The calculation for scope must be accurate, and;
- The percentage of loss of the anchor's holding power, due to the shorter scope, must be accurately calculated.

While you can often use this exception safely when the weather is mild, as the wind becomes stronger, the seas build, or the protection from seas is less than great, the risk of using this technique increases significantly. It is one of those techniques in the category of "maybe okay for mild conditions, but best ignored when conditions worsen".

STEM FITTINGS

One way to reduce the length of rode required, while maintaining adequate scope, is to use a snubber, attaching it to a fitting on the boat's stem as close to the waterline as is practical. However, caveats apply:

- Side-loading this fitting, which occurs when the boat veers, can cause it to break or deform with up to half the load that it is rated for in straight-line pull. To counter this weakness, the fitting should be more than twice as strong as it would need to be if only straight-line pull was involved. The strength of its fasteners should be least thrice that of the maximum load.

ROUND TURNS with ROLLING HITCH

- If the snubber is dead-ended at this fitting, to adjust or slip the rode, the rode must first be recovered enough for the crew to be able to reach the snubber where it is attached to the rode. This is inconvenient at best,

127

but when time is of the essence, the time required to do so can be critical. Instead, it is better if the snubber is lead to the stem fitting, then turned in some non-chafing manner, to be lead fair up to be belayed within reach from on deck. Then, the snubber can be adjusted, or if necessary, slipped.

- Snubbers are best belayed in a manner that allows for easy and controlled release while under a load. A cleat hitch, even if slipped, is not the best belay for this purpose since it can bind under a load. Instead, whether on a cleat, Samson post, bitt, piling, or other item, consider using a round turn or two, finished with a rolling hitch thrown around the line's standing part.

OTHER HALF OF THE EQUATION

Knowing how much line to deploy is only half of the "scope equation". The other half is knowing how much rode has actually been paid out. To do this you need to mark your rode. The marks must be easily seen and their meanings easily remembered. If they can be seen, or better

IDEA FOR 50'
MARK
SMALL STUFF
WHIPPED IN PLACE

IDEA FOR 100'
MARK
WHIPPINGS
AROUND THE
RODE

yet, felt in the dark, so much the better. Place them on the rode at pre-measured intervals, say every 25 feet; once the 100 foot mark is reached, the marking sequence can start over. There are also meters that can be attached to a windlass which will measure the amount of rode run out. For ideas other than those illustrated, ask boaters around any marina what works for them.

DEEP WATER ANCHORING

You will sometimes hear that in "deep" water, less scope can be used. Yes, this is true, as little as 3:1. But, the problem with this approach is that no one defines "deep", nor do they provide the parameters for maximum wind speed, or the maximum acceptable height of seas. When we've discussed this topic with offshore fishermen

> **HOW MUCH RODE TO HAVE ONBOARD**
> If you subscribe to our thinking, it should be clear that you need to carry onboard enough rode to enable the crew to deploy as many anchors as may be necessary, and do so with adequate scope for each anchor in the deepest water in which the boat will be anchored. Keep in mind that scope of 10:1 is often justified, and in some conditions, more than 10:1 may be required.

who routinely anchor in "deep" waters, they overwhelmingly support the need for more scope as the wind picks up, even if anchored in "deep" water.

Anchoring does not have to be an esoteric art; at times, hard, dirty, and wet maybe, but simple in its application. You need an anchor of the right design for the bottom, sized appropriately to the boat for the highest potential wind speeds and seas. Include good anti-chafe techniques, more than enough scope, and you will probably beat Mother Nature with her quirky sense of humor.

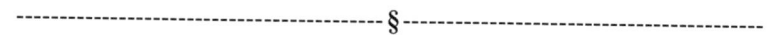

What about that boat in the Bahamas that we mentioned at the beginning of this chapter, how was that situation resolved? Since this boat had no other rope or chain onboard that was suitable for use as a rode, we combined his two separate rodes into one, and using the bigger of the two anchors, got him re-anchored.

Since only one anchor was deployed and the anchor design was far from ideal for the type of bottom, we encouraged the skipper to dive on the anchor to make certain it was dug in, and as the wind continued clock around, to periodically dive on the anchor to ensure that the anchor wasn't getting ready to trip.

Even though the water was warm and shallow enough to do this, being night, thus dark, made the job significantly more difficult–not an ideal solution. Fortunately, it all worked out just fine… this time.

EXAMPLES - CHAPTER 8

In this, and where applicable, in other chapters, examples relevant to the chapter's topic will be presented. All of the examples will be based on a hypothetical 35 foot sailboat, modest in windage, anchored where it has moderate protection from seas and with the freedom to oscillate.

In these examples, to provide an allowance for errors or omissions, plus to have a little bit of rode left in reserve, calculating scope will be done using a figure of 15:1.

MAIN BOWER:

For the main bower, an arbitrary amount of 20 feet will be used to account for the depth of water, height of tide, and the boat's freeboard at the bow.

Example: *20 feet (depth) x 15 (scope) = minimum 300 feet of rode*

STORM ANCHOR:

For the storm anchor, an arbitrary amount of 30 feet will be used to account for not only the depth of water, height of tide, and the boat's freeboard at the bow, but also, as only an example, to account for storm surge, wave height, and depth of the anchor's bury.

Example: *30 feet (depth) x 15 (scope) = minimum 450 feet of rode*

ADDITIONAL DETAILS

- The rode for the main bower can be all chain, all rope, or a combination of both. However, the rode for the storm anchor is best if it is predominately rope, with chain in those areas that may be subjected to chafe.

- There is no harm in using an all chain rode for either anchor as long as a snubber is employed which has the appropriate strength,

131

percentage of stretch, and enough stretch-length (see Chapter 5).

- There should be one complete rode for each anchor onboard.

- These rodes can be left intact as one rode, or they can be broken up into smaller lengths, allowing for easier stowage or manhandling around the boat. When the need arises to combine any of these lengths, splicing, bending, or lashing them together are all options.

CHAPTER 9

ANTI-CHAFE TECHNIQUES

"It does no good to go, if you cannot stay put once there."

There is no denying that chafe is the enemy of rope, attacking with scarcely little provocation at every opportunity. Protection from chafe in all but the mildest of weather demands planning and effort. On the other hand, every dollar and every ounce of effort spent will be well worth it.

"Chafe" used in this chapter, as it relates to rope, means more than just wear, being cut, or getting hot enough to melt, it also includes weakening the rope due to the way it is lead.

Chafe comes from several causes, most of which will fall into one of these categories:

- When the boat's movement and the rope's movement are contrary to each other, resulting in the boat "sawing" on the rope;
- From dynamic stretch, which causes the rope's fibers to "saw" against one another, or on some other item;
- From repetitive stretch, which can cause enough heat for the fibers to melt;
- Tight turns or small radii.

Most of the techniques to combat "chafe" will fall into one of four categories: reduce, replace, cover, or transfer. Any one technique can be used individually or in combination with another, regardless of the category in which it is placed.

REDUCE- Lessen opportunities for a rope to chafe, be cut, melt or lose strength:

- Keep leads as fair as possible.
- Make angles and bends as large as possible.
- Make any radius over which a rope may lie as large as possible.
- Avoid sharp edges, and round over the ones that cannot be avoided.
- Keep surfaces smooth.
- Keep the rope from touching anything.
- If a rope must touch, with the exception of belaying points, make surfaces that it touches roll, such as leading the line through a block or over a roller.
- If the surface cannot roll, surface the item that the rope touches with a slippery material, such as starboard, Teflon, Delrin, or other High Density Molecular Plastic (HDMP) with well eased edges. Wood can also be used; being sacrificial, the wood will wear instead of the rope.
- Reduce friction by lubricating surfaces that the rope touches with water, candle wax, synthetic grease, petroleum jelly or other lubricant that is compatible with the material from which the rope is manufactured, renewing the lubricant as needed.

> **RUNNING SNUBBERS THROUGH A BLOCK**
>
> Boats that have a bow sprit supported with standing rigging can hang a block from the bottom lug on the krantz iron. We have yet to find that this arrangement chafes the snubber on the bobstay unless it runs over sharp or rough edges. For other boats, an arch, possibly stainless steel or aluminum pipe, can be fabricated and installed at the bow, from which the block will hang, and through which the snubber is run. This installation requires that it be well supported against downward and lateral loads.

- Place cleats as close as possible to chocks or hawse holes in order to minimize the amount of "stretch length" available within this interval.

- Form a loop in the end of the rope, so that when doubled over a cleat, or around other belaying points, both legs of this loop will extend beyond the point of chafe, allowing the load to be shared by both legs, thus reducing stretch which might otherwise encourage the rope to chafe.

- To keep chafe off the rode on coral, rocks, engine blocks, or other objects lying on the bottom to a minimum, attach and position a float, adjusting its pendant for length, such that the rode rides above any obstruction. Be aware that lifting the rode off of the seabed can affect the rode-to-bottom angle at the anchor. As the wind speed rises, if maintaining a low rode-to-bottom angle is critical, you may need to dispense with this technique and, if necessary, relocate the vessel so that the rode is not at risk for rubbing on any of these items resting on the bottom.

REPLACE- Substitute a more chafe-resistant material for one that is more prone to chafe:

- Hard laid rope resists chafe better than soft laid rope.
- 3-strand, 8-plait (brait), and 12-braid rope resists chafe better than double braid rope.
- Polyester (Dacron) rope resists chafe better than Nylon rope.
- Larger diameter rope resists chafe better than smaller diameter rope.
- Wire rope or chain resists chafe better than fiber rope.
- HMPE (Dyneema/Spectra) and Aramid (Technora/Kevlar) ropes

resist chafe better than Nylon or polyester rope, but their very low stretch and low resistance to heat might influence their use.

Material	Critical Point (F)	Melting Point (F)
Aramid	520°	960°
Polyester	356°	450°
Nylon	325°	450°
HMPE	130°	390°

- Different lengths of rope can be jointed together with little risk of chafe at the join by splicing them together or by using interlocking eyes (Interlocking eyes Figure 1495, *The Ashley Book of Knots*). These eyes can be spliced in or formed by the use of any appropriate knot.

COVER- Install protective material around the rope in chafe prone areas:

- Some of the best protective materials to use against chafe are: leather (7 oz. or thicker), cotton duck (10 oz. or heavier), or polyester tubing. Polyester tubing is available at many locations where they make up hydraulic hoses. There are also a few high tech materials which, because they are tube-like, can be slid over the rope to provide protection.

- When harsh or prolonged conditions are expected, consider installing more than one layer of protective material. Each layer will install easier if it is generously oversized, relative to the thickness of the layer under.

- Install protective materials early because it may not be safe or even possible to do so once the wind picks up.

- Use long lengths of protective material and fix it in position so it cannot move. The more severe or active the boat's or the rope's movement, the longer this protective material should be. For harsh conditions, we favor protective material that is 16 inches or longer.

- When safe to do so, reposition protective material if wear appears.

- Any areas of restriction in which the rope will lie, areas such as rollers, chocks, or hawse holes, must be large enough to accommodate all of the layer(s) of protective material that might be installed. If those items are not large enough, replace or alter them.

- Water that penetrates to the rope aids in lubricating and cooling the fibers of the rope, so it is preferential to use water-porous materials.

- Some materials, notably fire hose, garden hose, and PVC tubing, inhibit the penetration of water to the rope, and have a high co-efficient of friction on their inner surface. This means that when the rope rubs back and forth on the inside, the rope's temperature will

> **FIRE HOSE - GARDEN HOSE - PVC TUBING**
> The concern over chafe occurring on the inside of these items may be more of a theoretical concern. Many boaters, mooring field and marina managers who use PVC tubing, garden hose, or fire hose for chafe protection often report little or no chafe or melting on lines. On the other hand, we have observed chafe and melting on lines that did spend time within these items. Whether or not to use these items is a decision that we'll leave up to you.

rise and can do so enough to reach the point that the rope's fibers will melt. If a high friction material must be used, keep the rope as wet as possible, even to the point of pouring water down the hose or tubing to help lubricate and cool the rope.

TRANSFER- Move the chafe onto other items or to other areas:

- Install snubbers—it is better to have the snubber chafe than the rode.

- If chafe will be unavoidable, install a back-up snubber(s).

- A rope which is subject to chafe, be it a rode or a snubber, should periodically be eased out– "freshening the nip". Do this well before the rope has sustained enough damage to allow it to part.

- If a dock line will be subjected to rough surfaces, as on cement pilings, for example, install a chafe resistant material around the item, or wrap a chain or large diameter line around it and then make the dock line fast to this attachment.

> **"FRESHENING THE NIP"**
> 1) To "freshen the nip", extra line must be available; better to have too much line, than too little. 2) The line must have been made fast within reach. 3) One of the best belays that allows for a safe and controlled easing or release of a rope that will be under a load is to use a couple of round turns, secured with a rolling hitch (see Chapter 8).

CHAPTER 10

CONNECTORS

"When anchoring, it is best to be conservative."

Hundreds of years ago when chain was first manufactured it was quickly adopted for shipboard use, and onboard seamen turned to their peculiar skills of knotting, hitching, and splicing to make connections to this new stuff. Those very same knots, hitches, and splices continue to be used even now-a-days, and a sailor from the 1600s would, even today, recognize these connections, though a few new ones have been added to the repertoire thanks to the emergence of some newer forms of rope.

However, today it is mostly metal connectors that are used to connect to chain. These come in a bewildering variety of sizes and shapes, many manufactured to specific grades of strength, so that the strength of the connector can match the strength of a chain to which it'll be connected, for example, "Grade 30" connectors, with Grade 30 chain, or "Grade 43" connectors, with Grade 43 chain. Though connectors are rated for strength, manufacturers do not give a Grade "X" rating to their connectors, but we have taken the liberty of referring to them as such in order to emphasize their strength, or lack thereof.

Keep these points in mind:

- Pick your connectors by matching their Work Load Limit (WLL) to that of the chain they'll be used with. Proof Loads and Breaking Loads should never be used to size connectors.

- Connectors can be made to any one of several worldwide-accepted manufacturing standards. When applicable manufacturing standards are followed, connectors and chain made to corresponding standards, if they are of the same size and grade, will fit together and be equal in strength. However, components made to one standard may not match chain made to another. (In the USA, the manufacturing standard for connectors is Federal Spec-RR-C-271-E.)

- Connectors can also be manufactured to less rigid requirements than those found in an accepted manufacturing standard, having dimensions or strength that is not suitable for use with the rest of the gear in the ground tackle.

- Connectors found in most chandleries or on store shelves are usually equal in strength to Grade 30 chain. Being "Grade 30" in strength, these connectors are not suitable for use with Grade 43 chain.

- Connectors are rated for straight-line pull. When a side-load is applied, a connector can break with a load as low as half its rated strength. When side loads are anticipated, choose a connector with a greater WLL, at least one size larger. If you choose a larger connector, you may also need to increase the size of the chain in order for it to fit the larger, stronger connector.

- Many connectors depend on a pin to make the join: 1) Such pins are usually of a higher strength metal. A replacement pin must have the same strength as the original pin; do not use just any old bolt. 2) If the connector might be subjected to side-loads, its pin must be threaded; plus, 2a) The pin should have some mechanism, such as the ability to use seizing wire (aka: mousing), to prevent it from backing out; and, 2b) To minimize corrosion, or with stainless steel, galling, the pin's threads should be coated with an agent to keep them lubricated and corrosion free. Ultra Tef Gel, anhydrous lanolin, petroleum jelly, synthetic grease, plumber's grease, or one of Forespar's proprietary products are some of the products that can be used for this purpose.

- Ungalvanized connectors can be coated with any one of the many rust-inhibiting products that are available; all of these products will require periodic re-application.

- For marine use, hot dipped galvanizing (HDG) is the finish of choice. Some connectors come with a standard thickness of galvanizing. Others may be double-dipped, in other words, kept in the molten zinc for a longer period of time, resulting in a thicker coating of zinc being deposited. Double-dipping provides for a longer service life.

- Sometimes plain or painted steel connectors can be galvanized. Before doing this, however, you should address these concerns: 1) Consult the manufacturer to determine whether the item will lose strength from the high temperatures (850°F) involved in the galvanizing process, or if necessary, from drilling out holes prior to galvanizing to allow for the thickness of the layer of zinc. 2) Holes may fill with zinc during the galvanizing process, but if the item is "spun" after being dipped in the zinc, the holes often empty of this excess zinc. However, not every galvanizing plant is equipped for "spinning", nor is it always completely successful. 3) If excess zinc remains in a hole, the hole will need to be drilled out, though this may inadvertently remove enough zinc for bare metal to be exposed. When that happens you have to resort to applying a rub-on, spray-on, or brush-on rust-inhibiting coating until the item is re-galvanized.

> **TIP:** When you have a small quantity of items to be galvanized, often the most economical approach is to piggy-back onto a larger load. This can sometimes be done with the cooperation of a local manufacturer that builds trailers, boat-lifts, anchors, or other products that need to be galvanized.

SHACKLES

Shackles are available in a bow (anchor) configuration or "D" (chain) configuration. Both types are available as regular-strength (carbon) shackles, designed to fit and equal in strength Grade 30 chain, or as high-strength (alloy) shackles, designed to fit and at least equal in strength Grade

ANCHOR SHACKLE

CHAIN SHACKLE

43 chain. Both are vulnerable to deformation or failure at loads lower than their given ratings when side loads are applied to them. High-strength (alloy) shackles, as well as the "chain" style shackles, are often an "order only" item, so be certain to order them early, long before that storm develops.

A shackle's pin is larger than the designated size of the shackle. For shackles manufactured to a worldwide-accepted standard, in smaller sizes this is usually one step higher. For example, a ½ inch shackle will have a ⅝ inch diameter pin. Alloy shackle pin heads are embossed with "HS".

Stainless steel shackles are also available, only some of which will have both the dimensions and strength that are compatible with G3 chain, and none that have the dimensions and strength that are compatible with G4 chain.

There are also shackles that have not been manufactured to an accepted standard, resulting in shackles that may not have the dimensions or strength that is necessary. It is important to investigate and understand the dimensions and strength of the shackle being considered.

Also, please review the caution that is boxed at the end of Chapter 2 concerning a shackle's WLL.

> **TIP:** To avoid stab wounds from those poky ends of mousing wire, once sufficient turns of the wire have been taken around the shackle, twist the ends of the wire together. Then, using needle-nose pliers, bend this twisted-together-tail down and sneak the ends under the turns of the mousing wire, thus placing these ends between the turns of wire and the body of the shackle, out of reach of rope, sails, and fingers.

OVERSIZED LINKS

Although they're not often seen in ground tackle, oversized links can be a valuable asset when installed in Grade 43 chain. Though High strength (alloy) shackles are made for use with Grade 43 chain, these shackles are not always readily available. However, with an oversized 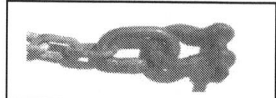 link installed you can also use regular-strength (carbon) shackles, one with a WLL equal to that of the chain, an advantage when trying to locate a shackle in poorly stocked chandleries.

Grade 43 chain is available with oversized links installed by the factory, often only by special order. But, oversized links can also be installed locally by a welder or machine shop, some with the mobile capability to come to your boat. This idea was suggested to us years ago by Frank Luke, of the Luke Anchor fame, and is one that we have been using successfully ever since. To do so:

- Use the largest diameter rod that will fit through the chain's link.

- Size the link so that once in place, its width will be wide enough to accept the shackle's pin, and its length will be long enough to accept the eye of the shackle.

- Once formed, the link is inserted into the chain, closed and welded shut.

- This link can be kept painted or coated with a rust inhibitor until the chain goes to be re-galvanized.

- In the event that any cracks develop while the link is being formed, the cracks should be ground out and welded up.

Stainless steel rod can also be used to make oversized links, and the good news is that these links are not at risk for galvanic corrosion. But, since stainless steel does carry the risk of pitting and crevice corrosion close inspections of these links is important, as is replacement the minute that any question as to their condition arises. Because of this risk, oversized links made from stainless steel rod are not well suited for anchor chain that will be used in oxygen starved environments.

CONNECTING LINKS

Connecting links are metal connectors that come in two halves, whereby each half has prongs that fit into corresponding holes in the opposing half.  When assembled, these prongs are cold-peened to hold the halves together. Most connecting links will be equal to their corresponding size of Grade 30 chain, though Campbell Chain Company (and possibly others) manufacture higher strength (alloy) connecting links, which matches in fit and equals in strength some sizes of Grade 43 chain. Connecting links are available in oval, as well as in pear-shaped configurations.

Some, but not all wildcats accommodate connecting links. If you expect to use a windlass, be sure to investigate compatibility before you install a connecting link. Depending on the manufacturer, connecting links are also called: missing links, replacement links, couplers or Koplers.

OTHER CONNECTORS

Several other types of connectors are also available. However, many are not galvanized, some have pins which are not threaded, most cannot be safety wired (moused), some come only in a "Grade 30" strength, many are not compatible with wildcats, or for other reasons, may not be suited for use in ground tackle. The four below are the more commonly available "other" connectors, none of which satisfy the requirements for use in ground tackle:

Twin Clevis	**Double Clevis**

Mechanical Couplers aka: Hammer Lock Couplers, Quick Coupling Links, Lok-A-Lok, Couplers, Kuplex Couplers, or component connectors. 	**Repair Links** These links are commonly found just about any place where chain is available, but they rarely even meet "Grade 30" strength, making them unsuitable for ground tackle. 

ROPE AS A CONNECTOR

Most mariners seldom consider rope as a connector, but it should not be overlooked as an economical and practical way to connect sections of chain. Strength-wise, it's no different than a rope-to-chain splice. Unless the rope must perform a specific service, such as use with a wildcat where the rope's diameter is usually twice that of the chain's size, the rope used is best sized so that its Work Load Limit, using a Factor of at least 8, matches as close as possible the WLL of the chain.

Although many knots and hitches can be used to connect rope to chain, splices are usually the most practical, strongest, and most secure. The splicing can be done in one of three manners: 1) Splicing the rope around a thimble, using a shackle to attach this combination to the chain. 2) Eliminating the thimble, splicing the rope directly to a shackle which is then connected to the chain. This is a more comfortable-on-the-hands option, than is choice #1, while still allowing the line to be disconnected from the chain. 3) If there is no need to disconnect the rope from the chain, splicing directly to the chain is a good option, one that will usually be necessary if the join will need to travel through a wildcat.

USING ROPE TO CONNECT TO CHAIN

When using a "rope connector", the shortest length of rope allowable is that which maintains a short length of unspliced rope between the ends of the two splices; there is no limit to the maximum length that is allowable, other than that which is dictated by the circumstances. Handling sections of chain joined together with rope also has the added advantage that it tends to be more pleasant on the hands, as compared to a join made with "hard" connectors, and even more so if those connectors have skin-poking ends of wire sticking out.

ROPE SPLICES

The following are the more popular of the splices used to connect rope and chain (Figure numbers refer to the illustrations in *The Ashley Book of Knots*):

146

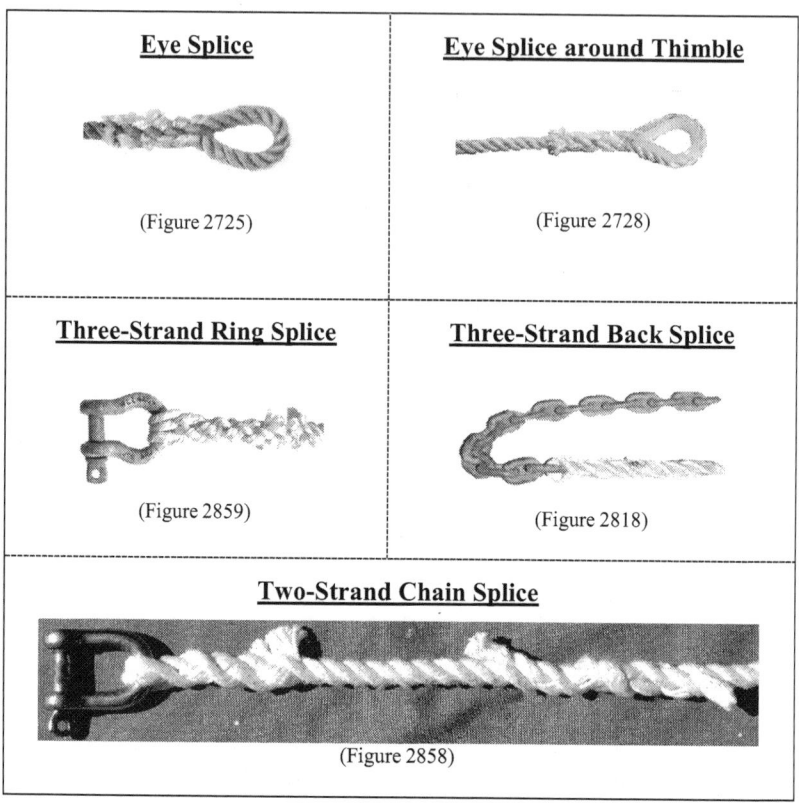

Eye Splice	**Eye Splice around Thimble**
(Figure 2725)	(Figure 2728)
Three-Strand Ring Splice	**Three-Strand Back Splice**
(Figure 2859)	(Figure 2818)

Two-Strand Chain Splice

(Figure 2858)

Although the Three-Strand Back Splice (not shown- Ashley's figure 2813, but with a shackle inserted between the strands at the point of the first set of tucks) is the easiest is to learn, the Two-Strand Chain Splice is most worthwhile to learn, as it produces the connection with the least girth while providing good strength and reliability if well made. This splice is particularly useful when the connection must run over a wildcat or through a deck pipe, chain stopper, or other narrow passage.

SPLICING TIPS

- For Nylon or polyester rope, a minimum of five tucks is necessary. More tucks do not provide more strength, but do provide more security.
- To avoid the splice backing out when not under a load, the throat should be cross-stitched or a whipping applied.
- The strands that are being tucked should be untwisted to lay flat as they go over the underlying strand.
- The last 2 tucks should be tapered by cutting out, prior to each tuck, 1/3 of the original number of yarns.
- When strands are cut or melted off, leave at least a rope's diameter of length remaining to allow for some pull-back as a load is applied.
- When the rope-chain splice will need to negotiate a wildcat, do not splice tight to the link, leave up to a pencil width (1/4" or a little bit less) of space where the strands go around the link in order for the splice's junction to be slack enough lay around the wildcat.
- The length of an eye splice should be a minimum of 3X the diameter of the object that it goes over; 5X the diameter is better.

CHOKE POINTS

Seldom will connectors be problematic when installed at the end of the chain. On the other hand, installed somewhere within the length of the rode, a connector can pose a big problem if a fitting that it must negotiate does not have enough clearance. If a bow roller, chain stopper, or deck pipe sized large enough to accommodate the connector is not available off-the-shelf, just about any machine shop or welder can fabricate a big-enough replacement. When made by local craftsmen, not only can these items be made bigger than their off-the-shelf cousins, they can be made heftier, too.

THINK OUTSIDE OF THE BOX

With some ingenuity, maybe something completely different can take the place of an original, too-small, ill-fitting, or poorly functioning item. For example, a short, stout line made fast to a Samson post or cleat, maybe around the base of the windlass, and attached to the rode with a rolling hitch, can substitute for a chain stopper.

CHAPTER 11

SWIVELS

The sound of shouting drew us up on deck where we watched the crew on another boat madly scurrying about in the rain and high winds, trying to get their boat re-anchored. The next day, being curious, we dinghied over to ask what had happened. In response, they held up a rope with half of a swivel still attached to its end. As we looked at what was remaining of the swivel, we realized that these folks had experienced the consequences of having installed their swivel on their anchor backward.

-------------------------------------- § --------------------------------------

Backward? Yes, backward! When the jaw of a galvanized jaw/eye swivel is attached directly to the anchor, that's "backward". Okay, so what's the danger?

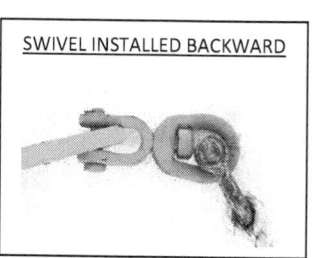
SWIVEL INSTALLED BACKWARD

When the anchor cannot remain in-line with the rode, the swivel can't either. This places a bending load on the "swivel mechanism", and when that happens, this pivot pin can break with less load than that for which it is rated, up to half as much. This is a significant point because side-loads on ground tackle are inevitable. While there are many different swivel designs, all have this same vulnerability to bending loads.

The broken swivel mentioned above is not an isolated incident, either. Over the years, we have seen enough broken swivels to realize that far too many boaters underestimate the danger that goes along with installing one of these commonly available jaw/eye swivels backward; and this becomes even more risky if the swivel is understrength to begin with.

JAW/EYE SWIVEL

If a swivel must be installed, consider using only eye/eye swivels. Eye/eye swivels require the use of shackles for their installation, making them impossible to install backward; plus, the shackles provide for at least a

EYE/EYE SWIVEL

modicum of universal movement at both ends of the swivel, further reducing the odds of the swivel being side loaded.

The best way to avoid a broken swivel is to avoid using one altogether. Unfortunately, this is not always practical because there are situations when using a swivel can be helpful. For example:

- When the boat is anchored where it will be subjected to more than a few cycles of reversing currents or clocking winds;
- When an anchor is of a design that has a tendency to spin when it is deployed or retrieved;
- As it is being retrieved the anchor needs to be rotated in order to be housed and this cannot be accomplished by giving the rode a twist at the roller or hawse pipe;
- When multiple anchors are deployed with rodes attached at a common point, such as a large ring, a swivel may prove beneficial when installed in-line between the ring and the pendant that leads to the boat.

MINIMIZE THE RISK

If a swivel needs to be installed, following a few rules-of-thumb can significantly reduce the odds of having the swivel break:

- The swivel must have a minimum Working Load Limit (WLL) that equals or exceeds the maximum load on the ground tackle. Unlike with shackles which have their WLL embossed on them, swivels do not. To establish the swivel's WLL, you will have to consult the manufacturer or their literature.

> **ADDITIONAL CAUTION WITH SWIVELS and OTHER CONNECTORS**
> Not only do jaw swivels carry the risk of being installed backward, they also have a more insidious danger. A swivel like this uses a clevis pin held in place by a cotter pin, instead of threads. This cotter pin can shear off, allowing the clevis pin to back out—an excellent reason to leave out of ground tackle swivels that depend on a non-threaded pin for their integrity. This danger with pins also pertains to any connector, not just swivels.

- For anchoring, only swivels with dimensions and strength that can be confirmed should be used. When manufactured to an accepted standard, a swivel's strength and dimensions are assured to be as required by the standards. That's not so if it's manufactured to a lesser or no standard. If you are forced to choose a swivel of questionable pedigree, consider up-sizing it to counter any potential for it to be weaker than what your requirements demand.

- To avoid side-loads on the swivel, each end of the swivel must have universal movement, in other words, they must allow movement unimpeded up and down and side to side. As mentioned, attaching a swivel to its adjacent partners using shackles provides at least a modicum of universal movement at each end of the swivel. But even better, a length of chain, or even just a few links, installed between the anchor and the swivel further decreases the odds of developing side-loads on the swivel.

SIDE LOADS UNAVOIDABLE

If you find yourself in a situation where a side-load on a swivel cannot be avoided, you do have a few options:

- Remove the swivel from the ground tackle, reinstalling it once the risk is gone.
- Switch to a bigger, stronger swivel, strong enough to resist breaking even when a bending load is applied to it.
- Deploy multiple anchors, each protecting the other(s) from any appreciable side-loads.

SWIVELS, CHAIN, AND THEIR SHACKLES

Attaching a swivel with a WLL that is equal to the chain is seldom a problem with G3 (Proof Coil or BBB) chain. This is because, if manufactured to a matching standard, regular-strength (carbon) shackles are designed to fit and match in strength G3 chain. This is not so with G4 (High Test) chain; with this chain, high strength (alloy) shackles must be used if the WLLs of the shackles will be equal to that of the chain. If regular-strength (carbon) shackles are to be used with G4 chain, for the shackles to fit and equal the chain in strength, the only option available is to have oversized links installed in the chain (see Chapter 10).

Remember, the question is not whether an understrength or improperly installed swivel has ever caused a problem in the past. Instead, ask yourself whether using it in the future will result in a problem.

> **STAINLESS STEEL SWIVELS**
>
> There are swivels manufactured from stainless steel, some with mechanisms that have wondrous universal movement. No matter how well-designed or machined, stainless steel swivels, too, are designed for straight line pull and will break with much less load when the swivel mechanism is placed under a side load. Even with this type of a swivel it pays to be careful and ask questions:
>
> - What is its strength in straight-line pull?
> - At what angle, however unlikely, will a side load or bending moment develop on its mechanism?
> - When side-loaded at what load will it break?
>
> If you are going to use a stainless steel swivel, use only those that conform to all of the recommendations listed in this chapter.

CHAPTER 12

TANDEM ANCHORS

In the Introduction, we told you about a time when we decided to ride out a hurricane at anchor because we thought that was a better option for keeping our boat safe. On that occasion, we decided to use tandem anchors.

Some considered anchoring in a storm of that severity foolish, and staying aboard even more so. But it worked, and the results speak for themselves. Our boat didn't drag, our gear didn't break or deform, and our rodes and snubbers didn't chafe. As to the seas that were generated over the miles of fetch, well, let's just say that they made life onboard miserable.

Another boat using tandem anchors in the same storm had very different results. In spite of being in a well-protected anchorage, it broke loose, causing havoc and damage all around the anchorage and sustaining extensive damage itself.

What made the difference between these two boats, where one stayed put and the other did not? When we recovered this other boat's ground tackle, it was clear that many of the protocols for using tandem anchors were violated. We think that the experience of this boat underscores the point that using tandem anchors is not as straightforward as it might appear.

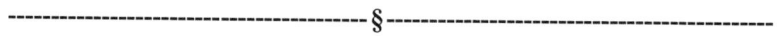

---------------------------------§-----------------------------------

"Tandem anchors is an arrangement where two anchors are attached to a single rode, one ahead of the other."

It is hypothesized that the increase in the holding power produced by tandem anchors is the result of the closer-in anchor plowing a trough in the bottom as it sets, which allows the more distant anchor that follows to set deeper once it reaches that now loosened-up trough. However, it could also be said that, unlike with two anchors which are deployed independently of one another, where the load is seldom carried simultaneously on both, with tandem anchors, once they have set, the load is more consistently carried by both anchors. We suspect that both explanations apply.

How much of an increase in holding power do tandem anchors provide? That depends on many factors, but the results from tests conducted by the U.S. Navy reveal that, *in mud* tandem anchors can increase the holding power by 20-30 percent, as compared to the same two anchors deployed individually. The difference is less in firmer bottoms.

Some of the protocols for the use of tandem anchors are the same, and are just as critical as those which apply to the use of any anchor:

- The anchors must be of the right design for the type of bottom in which they will be used;
- Each piece of gear's WLL must at least equal the highest load;
- Adequate scope must be deployed;
- Adequate swing room must be available;
- The main rode must be capable of adequately cushioning the surge loads, either on its own, or with a snubber or other mechanism installed.

But with tandem anchors, several other considerations also need to be addressed:

1. To be successful, tandem anchoring demands anchors of adequate size. In short, tandem anchoring should not be used as a substitute for undersized anchors.

2. The main rode, the one that leads from the boat, can be all chain, all rope, or a combination of both, and a snubber should be installed on whichever is used.

3. Secondary rodes are shorter lengths of rodes which attach the anchors to the main rode, or to one another. If possible, they should be made from a chafe resistant material. The less stretch in a secondary rode, the better, as then, more of the load is transferred to the anchor(s).

> **TIP:** Chain, wire rope, or large diameter polyester rope are good choices for a secondary rode, although there is nothing wrong with using large diameter Nylon rope.

4. Although there does not seem to be a "perfect distance" for spacing the two anchors, 15-20 feet between the two is a good rule of thumb. Too close together, and the secondary rode of the more distant anchor tends to interfere with the working of the closer-in anchor. And too far apart, it takes the more distant anchor longer to return to the furrow dug by the closer anchor after the boat has veered.

5. The two anchors used in tandem do not have to be the same in size or design, but each anchor must be able to set on its own in the type of bottom in which it is being used.

6. The more distant anchor must be of a design that can set with a zero rode-to-bottom angle. This is not so important for the closer-in anchor because the closer-in anchor can be set on a length of rode that is conducive to its setting before sufficient scope is veered for upcoming conditions.

7. Theoretically, the larger of the two anchors should be the closer-in

anchor, due to it having a higher rode-to-bottom angle, as compared to a zero rode-to-bottom angle on the more distant anchor. But our suspicion is that if sufficient scope is deployed, one that will result in a 6 degree rode-to-bottom angle, or less, this is a moot point.

> **SCOPE FOR TANDEM ANCHORS**
>
> Since tandem anchors are called into use when the weather turns harsh, keeping the rode-to-bottom angle to 6 degrees or less is important. This means that as the wind speed rises, especially beyond 25 knots, a 10:1 scope or more, could very well be required.

8. Even with tandem anchors, should one or both anchors trip, in the right circumstances even the best of anchors might not be able to reset on its own. If this is a possibility, about the only option available is to deploy two or more sets of ground tackle, either individual anchors or anchors in tandem, done so in such a manner that one will prevent another from tripping (see Appendix 7).

ARRANGING TANDEM ANCHORS

SINGLE SECONDARY RODE CONFIGURATION

In this configuration the more distant anchor's secondary rode is attached directly to the closer-in anchor, with the closer-in anchor being attached directly to the main rode.

Single secondary rode

Main rode

- It is critical that the more distant anchor's rode be attached to the closer-in anchor in a manner that does not interfere with the closer-in anchor's ability to set and hold. With the fisherman anchor, the secondary rode can wrap around the crown where the shank meets the

TANDEM ANCHORING LUG

LUG FOR TANDEM ANCHORING

arms. There are some anchors–stock-stabilized, pivoting fluke anchors, Navy stockless anchors, Rocna anchors, as well as a few other obscure designs–which have a lug or hole positioned specifically for attaching a tandem anchor.

- The rode from the more distant anchor should never be attached to the head of the closer-in anchor, nor to its shackle.

- Holes provided for trip lines are not in the correct position for attaching a second anchor in tandem. This hole is never to be used for attaching an anchor in tandem. If this is done, the closer in anchor will most likely trip.

- If an attachment from the more distant anchor to the closer-in anchor cannot be properly arranged, then the Double Secondary Rode configuration must be used.

DOUBLE SECONDARY RODE CONFIGURATION

In this configuration, each anchor has a secondary rode, each attached to the end of the main rode, usually to a large-enough ring or shackle. The closer-in anchor's secondary rode is about 2 feet in length, the more distant anchor's secondary rode being about 15-20 feet long.

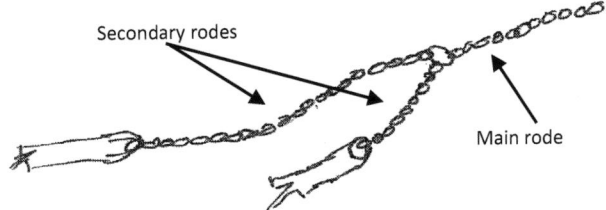

As a finale to this chapter, if tandem anchors are going to be used, all of the necessary gear should be gathered, checked for fit, altered or upgraded where necessary, and their deployment and retrieval is best practiced, all done months ahead of when the gear might be needed.

CHAPTER 13

BRIDLES

One winter, as we were anchored in a small cove waiting out a passing front, a trawler pulled in and anchored nearby. Once its anchor was set and the rode was paid out, the crew installed a bridle off the bow. Even with this bridle, the trawler kept shearing back and forth.

After an hour or so the owner came out and made a simple change that reduced the motion of the boat to almost nothing. He kept one leg of the bridle attached, but moved the opposing leg over to the same side, belaying it farther aft of the other leg, in this case, on a mid-ship cleat. Then, he adjusted the length on both legs until, almost magically, his boat started to lie sedately. There was little shearing back and forth of the boat for the remainder of his stay.

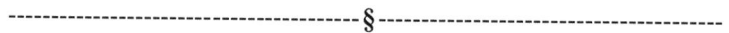

Bridles, also known as snubber bridles, anchor bridles, or riding bridles, are a popular topic with multi-hullers, as well as with trawler folk, but they can also be useful for other boaters. For all types of hulls bridles perform the same functions that a snubber performs—removing the load from the windlass mechanism, cushioning surge loads, and keeping any chafe that might occur off the rode. But, as our example shows, bridles can also be used to spring a boat in order to make the boat lie more comfortably to wind, waves, current, or tidal flow.

You can fashion a bridle in several ways:

- By attaching two single snubbers to the rode, belaying them to opposite sides of the bow; the rode is made fast but left slack.

- By attaching two separate snubbers to a fitting, usually one made of metal. This fitting is attached to the rode. The snubbers are belayed to opposite sides of the bow; the rode is made fast, but left slack. These metal fittings can only be used with a chain rode.

- By making up a Y-shaped bridle, the tail attached to the rode, either rope or chain, using a rolling hitch, and each leg belayed to opposite sides of the bow; the rode is made fast, but left slack.

THE CONUNDRUM

Some literature suggests that each leg of a bridle can be reduced to 70 percent of the strength of what a single snubber would have. But if you do this, when the boat veers and the pull is only on one leg of the bridle, that leg may not have the strength, stretch, or chafe resistance required. On the other hand, if each leg of the bridle is sized to equal the strength of a single snubber, when the boat is pulling equally on each leg, the combined strength may be too much, providing too little stretch and inadequately cushioning surge loads.

> **TIP:** In milder conditions, a bridle with a long tail can be hitched on "short", or a different bridle can be used, one with a shorter tail. But keep in mind, that if the conditions deteriorate, the former should have its tail let out, while the latter will need to be switched out for a bridle with a longer tail.

So how is this conundrum resolved? We think, especially for bridles for use in harsh weather, that the answer lies in the bridle's tail.

The entire bridle can be made from rope of a strength that would be chosen for a single-legged snubber, but the tail should be of Nylon rope and of long length, at least 30-40 feet. In this arrangement, whether the load is on one leg or both, all parts of the bridle are of adequate size to provide the strength that is needed, which also improves the chafe resistance of the line used. In harsh weather, it is the single, long, Nylon tail that will provide the stretch needed to cushion surge loads.

Another advantage to this arrangement is that the individual legs can be made from chafe-resistant material, such as polyester, chain, or wire rope, with the long tail made from Nylon for stretch.

THE WEAK SPOT

A bridle's weakness is its throat, the location where the two legs of the bridle join together; the wider the throat angle, the more susceptible the throat is to damage, even to the point of parting.

In mild conditions, since the load on the bridle is low, the angle at the throat can be as wide as 45-degrees, but a 45-degree throat angle left in place under a too-high load can result in damage to the rope's fibers, damage that is cumulative and permanent. Such damage can go undetected. When severe enough, this damage will allow the bridle to part, many times without warning, even parting at a later date during less severe conditions.

> **DETERMINING THE ANGLE AT THE THROAT**
> Mark the legs of the bridle at easy-to-remember intervals:
> a) If the length of the legs of the bridle is 1.3X the widest distance between the legs, the throat angle will be 45-degrees.
> b) If the length of the legs of the bridle is 2X that of the widest distance between the legs, the throat angle will be 30-degrees.

As conditions start to worsen, the angle of the throat needs to be smaller, no more than 30-degrees. Since there are no guidelines established to determine when use of a 30-degree throat angle should supersede using a 45-degree angle, common sense must prevail; establish a 30-degree throat angle early, rather than later.

CHAPTER 14

DEPLOYING and RETRIEVING ANCHORS

One calm day, we watched as a couple on a chartered sailboat came into the anchorage. She was at the helm, he was on the bow. Once he let go the anchor, the signal to back down was given. She put the boat in reverse–full throttle–and that chain came smokin' out of that chain pipe. Then, as the rode reached its limit, the boat fetched up hard, almost tossing that fella off the bow. Yes, that anchor had set, but they were very lucky that the chain, windlass, or some other piece of gear did not break.

---------------------------------------§---------------------------------------

Few boats come adequately outfitted with all of the necessary equipment and gear for anchoring in all conditions, or in any type of bottom that the crew might encounter. Making the boat so equipped should be a top priority for the new owner, and this includes the ability to deploy and retrieve the biggest, heaviest, or the most awkward-to-handle gear.

> **TIP:** Simplicity, flexibility, adaptability, and being innovative in thought as well as application are all important when it comes to deploying and retrieving anchors. Then, too, having all of the necessary gear onboard, to begin with, should go without the need to be said.

DEPLOYING

Good technique for deploying your anchor is as follows: First, position the boat, halt forward momentum, and as sternway is gained, lower the anchor to the seabed. Pay out some rode and set the anchor. Then, deploy an appropriate length of rode for the worst conditions that will exist until the anchor is raised. Install a snubber and secure the rode. Don't forget to hang the mandated day shape, or if night is coming on, the anchor light. (For instructions on how to set multiple anchors, see Appendix 7.)

OTHER THOUGHTS

- If the location is unfamiliar, enter slowly, checking for adequate depth and the absence of obstructions, including where the current or wind may later swing the boat.

- Deploying the anchor by just tossing it overboard, though rightly frowned upon, can be an option. But, when done, it's important to bring the anchor back to the surface to verify that it hasn't fouled, clear it if necessary, then proceed to lower and set it.

- To set the anchor use a scope of around 4:1, though this figure is an approximation. For hard bottoms, scopes of 7:1 or more may be necessary to get an anchor's flukes to dig in. In soft bottoms, some anchors, in order for their flukes to dig in need shorter scopes, 3:1 or even 2:1. In a rock bottom, no amount of scope will allow an anchor's flukes to dig into an impenetrable bottom like this.

- When setting an additional(s) anchor with the "big" boat is not practical, anchors can be taken out by dinghy. The dinghy can be rowed or powered, though with much wind or current, rowing might not be a viable option.

- When an anchor is deployed by dinghy, the rode can be towed away from the main vessel, though the drag on the rode may cause difficulties in positioning the anchor where desired. The other alternative is to load the entire rode into the dinghy, then position the dinghy where the anchor is to be dropped, drop the anchor, then pay out the rode from the dinghy as it returns to the main vessel. In this latter method, carrying a float or extra line in the dinghy could be helpful in case the rode comes up short.

- Two or more dinghies working in tandem can be used to deploy an anchor. The anchor is worked from one dinghy, while the other provides power and steerage. This is a particularly effective method to use when currents are running or the wind is strengthening.

- When getting additional anchors out by dinghy is just not practical or safe, consider using fenders, cushions, or enough other items with sufficient flotation to support the anchor and large loops of rode that follow. Then, using your mask, fins, and snorkel, swim the gear out into place. In cold water, a wet suit might be a welcome addition to this gear. The anchor and rode need only to float high enough to keep them from dragging on the bottom. If the flotation pendants are attached with a slip, or slipped knot, the gear is easier to let go.

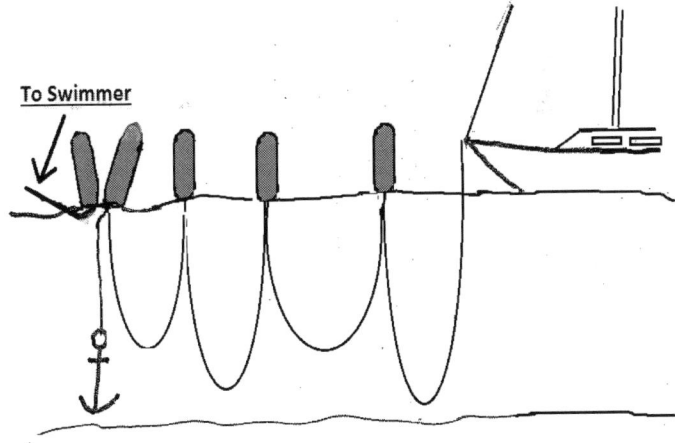

To Swimmer

- Getting an anchor of size overboard, one not housed on a roller or kept in a hawse pipe, may require a windlass or winch, a davit, or boom with associated tackle, turning blocks, or other contrivances, plus some ingenuity, and maybe an additional crew member(s).

- If the anchor may become fouled, prior to deploying it first attach a trip line (see Chapter 5) or scow the anchor (see Appendix 6).

RETRIEVING

- If an anchor, particularly a heavy or awkward-to-handle one, will need more than a minimal amount of time for retrieval, another anchor may need to first be deployed to hold the boat in position while the time is taken to retrieve the larger anchor.

- Although retrieving an anchor might, at times, need to be done quickly, it should not be done at the expense of safety. When weather or other conditions may complicate retrieving your gear, or make it unsafe to do so, consider postponing the retrieval until the conditions improve. Otherwise, consider buoying the rode, then slip it, recovering the gear at a later time.

- If the rode and anchor are to be manhandled, to avoid dings to the boat, protection of some type can be judiciously placed. We use 10 oz. canvas tarps, sized approximately 2' x 3', pieces of 1/4" plywood, sized approximately 8" x 8", or 1/8" pieces of rubber gasket material, size approximately 5" x 5"; boat cushions also work well.

- Retrieving an anchor is often easier if a trip line has been attached to the anchor. This trip line may be called upon to handle thousands of pounds of strain, especially when breaking out a deeply buried anchor. Half-inch rope is generally accepted as the smallest diameter, for "comfort", to use when retrieving an anchor by hand.

- Options for creating advantage over a too-heavy anchor can include such items as a windlass, winch, boom, davit, or cathead; all may require the use of messenger lines,

> **BOOMS**
> Remember, not all booms need to lead aft; if circumstances require, some booms are more practical if lead forward.

tackle, turning blocks, or other gear. Although "pretty" is not a requirement for the arrangements, function and results are.

- Whether you are setting or breaking out an anchor, to avoid damaging a windlass, a chain stopper or a short, stout snubber can be beneficial in that they can be used to remove the load from the windlass mechanism, a load which can reach into the thousands of pounds. If you're using a snubber, whether short or long, it can be belayed to any point that is strongly installed and practical in its location; the working end of this snubber can be attached to the rode simply by using a rolling hitch.

RETRIEVING DEEPLY BURIED ANCHORS

In soft bottoms an anchor under load can bury to considerable depths, where recovering it may be problematic. In these situations, maintaining a strain on the rode and giving the anchor time to work itself to the surface often works. Seas, waves, and wakes, along with some sternway will often work to your advantage in retrieving deeply buried anchors.

When this fails, another retrieval technique to consider is to play on a weakness of many anchors–that of tripping when side loaded. Try veering the boat 30-degrees or more, maybe to one side then the other while attempting retrieval. In either case, many times a substantial load on the rode may be involved.

However, it's generally cautioned by anchor manufacturers to not power forward beyond the anchor, as in this direction anchors are more vulnerable to bending or breaking.

ANCHOR LIGHTS AND DAY SHAPES

The following rules are compulsory; with compliance, other vessels are put on notice, that the vessel displaying the round, black day shape or the all-round, white light is anchored, thus: 1) Does not have the ability to maneuver; 2) Has at least one anchor rode, and possibly other gear deployed; and, 3) Vessels maneuvering in the vicinity are required to avoid a collision with the anchored vessel.

On the other hand, not properly displaying the appropriate shape or light places the onus for any collision, if not totally, at least partially, on the anchored vessel.

The following are direct quotes from the rules, and are offered for your contemplation:

COLREGS Rule 30 (International Rules) and 33 CFR 83.30 (USA Inland Rules)- "(a) A vessel at anchor shall exhibit where it can best be seen (i) in the fore part, an all-round white light or one ball; (ii) at or near the stern and at a lower level than the light prescribed in subparagraph (i), an all-round white light. (b) A vessel of less than of less than 50 meters in length may exhibit an all-round white light where it can best be seen instead of the lights prescribed in paragraph (a) of this rule. (e) A vessel of less than 7 meters in length, when at anchor, not in or near a narrow channel, fairway or anchorage, or where other vessels normally navigate, shall not be required to exhibit the lights or shape prescribed in paragraphs (a) and (b) of this rule".

An exception to the above rule, applicable only to USA Inland Rules, is 33 CFR 83.30 (g) which states- "A vessel of less than 20 meters in length, when at anchor in a special anchorage area designated by the Coast Guard shall not be required to exhibit the anchor lights and shapes required by this rule". (*The few so designated anchorages in existence can be found in the region's applicable Coast Pilot.*)

COLREGS Annex I-9-(b) (i) (*International Rules*) and 33CFR 84.15 (b) (*USA Inland Rules.*)- "All-round lights shall be so located as not to be obscured by masts, topmasts or structures within angular sectors of more than 6 degrees, except anchor lights prescribed in Rule 30 which need not be placed at an impracticable height above the hull".

COLREGS Annex I-9-(b) (ii) (*International Rules*) and 33CFR 84.15 (c) (*USA Inland Rules*)- "If it is impractical to comply with paragraph (b) (i) of this section by exhibiting only one all-round light, two all-round lights shall be used suitably positioned or screened so that they appear, as far as practical, as one light at a distance of one mile".

COLREGS Annex I-11 (*International Rules*) and 33CFR 84.17 (*USA Inland Rules*)- Intensity of non-electric lights–"Non-electric lights shall so far as practical comply with the minimum intensities, as specified in the table given in Section 8 of this Annex".

CHAPTER 15

THE SLIDING SCALE FOR ANCHORS, GEAR & SCOPE

PUT IT ALL TOGETHER

So what's a captain to do to get his boat and his ground tackle ready to begin anchoring in earnest? Here are a few recommendations:

- Make an honest and practical evaluation of which types of bottoms you expect to encounter. Then choose the types of anchors that you believe are most suitable. If you are debating sizes, go with the larger size anchor. Table 6- Anchor Comparisons, provides a simplistic overview of the anchors discussed in these chapters, but you should not use this table alone. Take into account all the subtleties and nuances of anchor performance as discussed in Chapters 6 and 7.

- Survey every piece of your boat's ground tackle—anchors, chain, fiber rodes, shackles, swivels, snubbers, bow rollers, windlass, strong points such as a Samson post, bitts, or cleats, anti-chafing gear, and all else. Make a list of what you need to add, up-grade, or replace, with special attention to avoiding weak links. Then set about acquiring your gear. Remember, you want everything in the ground tackle to be strong enough for the heaviest demands that it will encounter, and be onboard before the need is present. Don't compromise.

- Make whatever additions or alterations are needed for your boat, and likely, its dinghy. You need to be able to deploy, set, snub, retrieve, and stow this ground tackle with as little difficulty as possible. Don't just make do, instead make good choices.

- Rig your gear, practice, and experiment with it. You'll learn from your practice, and you'll become more capable at anchoring your boat safely in different conditions. It is time well spent.

LOOKING FOR A BOAT?
Those doing so should ask themselves: How much money can I allocate to equip the boat with a full complement of ground tackle, what is the largest size anchor that both the crew and I can manhandle, and what equipment will be necessary to handle it in the harshest weather that we can encounter? Then, based on this complement of equipment and ground tackle, working backward, you can establish the biggest size boat that you might want to consider owning.

THE SLIDING SCALE

Up to this point choosing and using your ground tackle has been presented as being cut and dried, or maybe black and white. In reality, there will be times when, because of variables that are out of your control, it will be neither.

That is when the following chart, the *Sliding Scale for Anchors, Gear & Scope*, will be useful to help you balance these variables with one another. An admonishment that bears repeating: a conservative approach should always be given to any decision concerning anchoring, and with this chart, that means favoring the

---

TIP: Anchoring, as well as other activities, are often done in rain; to prevent rainwater from running down your neck and soaking your shirt, wrap a towel around your neck, then, zip your jacket up around the towel.

"right" side of the chart. Although this chart covers the more important of the variables that may be involved in your decision, always remain alert for others, applying the same approach to them—a sliding scale, one which favors the "right" side, a "conservative" side.

SLIDING SCALE FOR ANCHORS, GEAR & SCOPE

POSSIBLY	MUST HAVE
SMALLER ANCHORS	LARGER ANCHOR
DIFFERENT ANCHOR DESIGN	MORE EFFECTIVE DESIGN
LESS STRONG GEAR	STRONGER GEAR
LESS SCOPE	MORE SCOPE

Sailboat / Less 30 knots / Mod protection / Oscillate / In sand

LOW WINDAGE	LOTS OF WINDAGE
LOW WIND SPEED	WIND SPEED RISING
NO SEAS or WAVES	SEAS or WAVES
FIRM BOTTOM or SAND	SOFT BOTTOM or MUD
FREEDOM TO OSCILLATE	CANNOT OSCILLATE
APPROPRIATE FLUKE ANGLE	INAPPROPRIATE FLUKE ANGLE

SLIDING SCALE FOR ANCHORS, GEAR & SCOPE

POSSIBLY

SMALLER ANCHORS

DIFFERENT ANCHOR DESIGN

LESS STRONG GEAR

LESS SCOPE

MUST HAVE

LARGER ANCHOR

MORE EFFECTIVE DESIGN

STRONGER GEAR

MORE SCOPE

Sailboat
Less 30 knots
Mod protection
Oscillate
Sand

Possibly	Must Have
SHORT DURATION	LONG DURATION
NO CURRENTS	CURRENTS
NO UNANTICIPATED LOADS	UNANTICIPATED LOADS
NO RESONANCE	RESONANCE
NO BENDING LOADS	BENDING LOADS
NO SHOCK LOADS	SHOCK LOADS

172

Wait, you are not done! Read through the following Tables and Appendices. Blend all the information together into a balanced system that will work for you and that will satisfy Mother Nature's requirements.

Since many of the subtleties and nuances throughout this book may have been missed, or by this point, forgotten, go back and reread it. Every time that a question or a problem with anchoring develops, reread it yet again.

When something does go wrong, figure out the problem(s) and correct it (them), always in a way that will beat Mother Nature. If you are not sure where to start looking for the answer(s), begin with "The Big 5 + multiple anchors".

> We salute your goal for
> "ZERO DRAGGING".

Table 1

ISO Chain

ISO Grade 30- Proof Coil

Size	WLL (lbs.)	Inside Width (inches)	Inside Length (inches)	Weight (lbs./ foot)
1/4	1300	.507	1.000	.73
5/16	1900	.507	1.100	1.09
3/8	2650	.620	1.230	1.55
1/2	4500	.820	1.500	2.50
5/8	6900	1.0	1.900	3.62
3/4	10,600	1.09	2.205	5.80

Data provided by Peerless Industrial Group (ACCO).

174

Table 1
ISO CHAIN

ISO Grade 30- BBB

Size	WLL (lbs.)	Inside Width (inches)	Inside Length (inches)	Weight (lbs./ foot)
1/4	1300	.43	0.87	.72
5/16	1900	.50	1.00	1.10
3/8	2650	.62	1.09	1.56
1/2	4500	.75	1.34	2.77

Data provided by Peerless Industrial Group (ACCO).

ISO Grade 43- High Test

Size	WLL (lbs.)	Inside Width (inches)	Inside length (inches)	Weight (lbs./ foot)
1/4	2600	.410	.845	.73
5/16	3900	.510	1.030	1.03
3/8	5400	.590	1.220	1.47
7/16	7200	.650	1.400	2.05
1/2	9200	.760	1.590	2.56
5/8	13,000	.900	1.790	4.21

Data provided by Peerless Industrial Group (ACCO).

Table 2

NACM Chain

NACM Grade 30- Proof Coil

Size	WLL (lbs.)	Inside Width (inches)	Inside Length (inches)	Weight (lbs./ foot)
3/16	800	.300	.98	.39
1/4	1300	.380	1.24	.65
5/16	1900	.440	1.29	1.00
3/8	2650	.550	1.38	1.36
7/16	3700	.650	1.64	2.10
1/2	4500	.720	1.79	2.30
5/8	6900	.790	2.20	3.70
3/4	10,600	.980	2.76	5.33
7/8	12,800	1.08	3.03	7.75
1	17,900	1.25	3.58	10.10

Data provided by the National Association of Chain Manufacturers.

Table 2

NACM CHAIN

NACM Grade 43- High Test

Size	WLL (lbs.)	Inside Width (inches)	Inside Length (inches)	Weight (lbs./ foot)
1/4	2600	.38	1.24	.70
5/16	3900	.44	1.29	1.06
3/8	5400	.55	1.38	1.54
7/16	7200	.65	1.64	2.05
1/2	9200	.72	1.79	2.67
5/8	13,000	.79	2.20	4.02
3/4	20,200	.98	2.76	5.67
7/8	24,500	1.08	3.03	7.75
1	26,000	1.42	2.87	10.10

Data provided by the National Association of Chain Manufacturers.

Table 2

NACM CHAIN

NACM Grade 70- aka: Transport or Binding Chain

Size	WLL (lbs.)	Inside Width (inches)	Inside Length (inches)	Weight (lbs./ foot)
1/4	3150	.38	1.24	.81
5/16	4700	.44	1.29	.98
3/8	6600	.55	1.38	1.41
7/16	8750	.65	1.64	2.16
1/2	11,300	.72	1.79	2.46
5/8	15,800	.79	2.20	3.47
3/4	24,700	.98	2.76	unknown

Data provided by the National Association of Chain Manufacturers.

Table 3

Stainless Steel Chain

STAINLESS STEEL CHAIN- NACM STANDARD

Size	WLL (lbs.)	Inside Width (inches)	Inside Length (inches)	Weight (lbs./ foot)
1/4	1570	.30	1.24	.57
5/16	2400	.38	1.29	.92
3/8	3550	.55	1.38	1.50
7/16	5400	.65	1.64	2.0
1/2	6500	.72	1.79	2.0
5/8	9800	.79	2.20	3.31
3/4	15,000	.98	2.85	5.0
1	23,250	1.25	3.58	9.0

Data provided by the National Association of Chain Manufacturers.

Dimensions for Stainless Steel ISO Proof Coil, BBB, and High Test chain sizes differ from the values listed in this table.

Table 4

Mooring Chain

MOORING CHAIN- aka: LONG LINK CHAIN

Size	WLL (lbs.)	Inside Width (inches)	Inside Length (inches)	Weight (lbs./ foot)
3/8	3700	.62	1.23	1.3
1/2	6000	.81	1.50	2.3
5/8	9000	.94	2.52	3.4
3/4	13,500	1.16	3.0	5.1

This data is for Mooring Chain manufactured by Peerless Chain Company (ACCO); other manufacturers' specifications may vary.

Table 5

Rope Sizes and Tensile Strengths

(Dimensions are for rope diameter):

Rope Size	Minimum Breaking Strength
¼ in.	1,486 lbs.
⅜ in.	3,240 lbs.
½ in.	5,670 lbs.
⅝ in.	8,910 lbs.
¾ in.	12,780 lbs.
⅞ in.	17,280 lbs.
1 in.	22,230 lbs.
1 ⅛ in.	28,260 lbs.
1 ¼ in.	34,830 lbs.
1 ½ in.	48,600 lbs.

This chart gives Minimum Breaking Strengths for 3-strand or 8-plait Nylon ropes manufactured to the Cordage Institute standards. Minimum Breaking Strength for 12-braid Nylon rope is approximately 8 percent higher.

Table 6

Anchor Comparisons

Anchor	Known For	Fluke Angle	Fluke Area	Good In	Worst In
Bruce, Claw	Hard to stow on deck	Shallow	Moderate	S,M,C,Ma,R,B	W
CQR	Pivotal shank	Shallow	Moderate	S,M,R,B	C,Ma,W
Danforth	High holding power	Shallow	Large	S,M,R,B	C,Ma,W
Delta	Fixed Shank	Shallow	Moderate	S,M.C,Ma,R,B	W
Fisherman	Excellent in weeds	Between shallow and deep	Moderate	Any bottom	N/A
Fortress	Extreme light weigh, high holding power	Adjustable-2 positions	Large	S,M,R,B	C,Ma,W
Navy Stockless	Hawse storage	Deep	Large	M,R,B	S,C,Ma,W
Northill	Large palms	Shallow	Large	S,M.C,Ma,R,B	W
Pekny	Changeable palms	Shallow	Variable	S,M.C,Ma,R,B	W
Rocna*	"Roll bar"	Shallow	Moderate	S,M.C,Ma,R,B	W
Spade**	Heavy tip	Shallow	Moderate	S,M.C,Ma,R,B	W
Super MAX	High holding power	Adjustable-3 positions	Large	S,M.C,Ma,R,B	W

TABLE 6

ANCHOR COMPARISION TABLE

* Rocna anchor category includes Rocna, Mantus, Manson Supreme or other roll bar scoop anchors
** Spade anchor category includes Spade, Manson Boss, Rocna Vulcan or other non-roll bar scoop anchors
*** Shallow and Deep fluke angles relate to the terms as used in Chapter 6
**** Anchors must be sized as outlined in Chapter 6 and 7

BOTTOM CHARACTERISTICS		
B= Boulders	Ma= Marl	W= Weeds
C= Clay	R=Rocks	
M= Mud	S= Sand	

Appendix 1

OTHER LOAD TABLES

In addition to the table used in Chapter 3, other approaches to calculating the loads on ground tackle include: ABYC's table, Robert Smith's table, and the Wind Drag Formula.

Regardless of which approach is used, when calculating the load on the ground tackle, the reader must: 1) Be cognizant of the parameters that apply to the data; 2) Be aware that the gear must be appropriately sized to this data; and, 3) Understand that the gear should not be used in conditions that extend beyond the parameters that apply to the data.

The ultimate responsibility for establishing the load on the ground tackle, and the consequences that result, good or bad, rests with the vessel's owner or possibly its operator.

ABYC TABLE

ABYC's table includes the data for wind speed, surge loads, and current drift for traditional-sized and shaped sailboats, anchored with moderate protection from seas, and the boat having the freedom to oscillate. Tom Hale, a past technical director at ABYC, told *Practical Sailor Magazine* that the figures in the ABYC's table also include a hefty, though unknown Safety Factor. Robert Taylor PE, though, has since calculated that the ABYC table includes a Safety Factor of three. With this in mind and comparing these figures to the load figures in Chapter 3, it appears that this table is based on winds speeds of around 30-knots. It should also be noted that the ABYC table is titled as "Design Loads", not "Wind Loads". For 60 knot winds, multiple the figures in the ABYC table by four.

ROBERT SMITH'S TABLES

These tables show actual wind loads recorded on both sail and power boats anchored in a river with a fetch of 4 miles. This data does not include surge loads. We don't know whether this data was obtained using vessels with more windage than that of a "traditional" sailboat, nor whether the boat was free to oscillate. We have to assume that current drag on the boat was present, but we do not know the amount, though we can assume that it was rather insignificant.

WIND DRAG FORMULA

The standard wind drag formula provides for wind loads, along with surge and current drag loads, on a boat, with the wind having a zero angle of attack relative to the boat. One of these formulas is provided in *The Complete Book of Anchoring and Mooring*, by Earl Hinz, where he has expanded the formula to include a wind angle of attack on the boat of 30-degrees, resulting in data which is more realistic, and which closely mirrors the data provided in Chapter 3.

Appendix 2

LOCKER, BIN & DECK PIPE SIZES

LOCKER AND BIN SIZES FOR CHAIN

A rough estimate of space needed to store a length of chain can be approximately calculated using this formula:

Length of chain in feet x (chain size)^2 ÷ .9 = minimum cubic feet of space needed (estimate only).

For example:

100 feet of ¼ inch chain- 100 x .25 x .25 ÷ .9 = 6.9 cu ft.

LOCKER AND BIN SIZES FOR ROPE

A rough estimate of space needed to store a length of rope can be approximately calculated using this formula:

Rope length (feet) x (rope diameter)^2 ÷ 6 = minimum cubic feet of space needed (estimate only).

For example:

200 feet of ½ inch rope- 200 x .5 x .5 ÷ 6 = 8.3 cubic feet.

–or–

For tightly packed rope- rope circumference (inches) x length of rope (feet) x 1.6= minimum cubic feet required (estimate only).

For randomly packed rope- rope circumference (inches) x length of rope (feet) x 2.0= minimum cubic feet required (estimate only).

DECK PIPE SIZES FOR CHAIN

- The minimum inside diameter should be 8x the chain diameter.

- In order to provide for the rode to drop unimpeded, there should be a minimum of 18 inches from highest level of chain to bottom of pipe; 24 inches of clearance is better.
- Flaring of the bottom of the pipe is unnecessary if there is a minimum of 24 inches of clearance between it and the top of the pile, and if the pipe is inclined 10° or less.
- The pipe should not incline more than 45°.

DECK PIPE SIZES FOR ROPE

- The minimum inside diameter should be 7.5 x rope diameter.
- In order to provide for the rode to drop unimpeded, a minimum of 18 inches of space should remain from top of the pile of rope to the bottom of the deck pipe; 24 inches of clearance is better.
- Flaring the bottom of a deck pipe is unnecessary if there is a minimum of clearance between it and the top of the pile, and if the pipe is tilted less than 10 degrees.
- Pipe should not be tilted more than 45 degrees.

Appendix 3

HOW TO THROW A ROPE

The ability for each crew member to competently throw a line is an extremely helpful skill, since many times it is not convenient or even possible for one crew member to stop what they are doing to throw a line for another. Fortunately, learning to throw a line is a skill that is easily and quickly learned.

THE TECHNIQUE

To throw a line, coil the line in one hand, then divide these coils between both hands, avoiding tangles. Swinging the coils from your side, release the coils from the leading hand first,

> **TIP:** If folks are having to struggle to catch your line, the line is probably too short. Instead, throw longer lines, at least 30 feet long; for larger boats, 40 feet or more will probably be needed.

followed a fraction of a second later by letting go the coils in the other hand. Don't forget to hold onto the bitter end of the line. (See pictures on back cover.)

- Whether for the first try or a repeat, take the time to coil the line properly before it is thrown.

- Aim to the immediate side of the person to whom you're throwing. If you must aim at the person, throw the line above their head, allowing the line to fall on the catcher. That's much less painful for them, than getting hit directly in the face with the coils of rope.

- It may be best not to belay the bitter end of the line until after it has been caught, as the belay will shorten the length of available line to throw.

- For throwing, ½ inch diameter line seems to be the best all-around size, but ⅝ inch may be required for better carry. Three-eighths inch line may be too light for all but the shortest tosses; it's also uncomfortable on the hands when the line is placed under any but the lightest load.

- If a little more weight is needed in the end of the line, say to give the line more carry, simply tie an overhand knot in the end of the line; if even more weight is needed, add more turns to the knot. For those with the interest or skill, a monkey fist can be made up and used.

- Since an eye in a thrown line can interfere in a myriad of ways, it is often better to throw bare-ended lines–lines without a loop or eye.

- The person catching the line does not need to know how to tie a knot, or to even speak the same language. Just point from the person who you want to catch the line to where you want the line belayed. Toss the line to them, then, making circles with one of your fingers, encourage the person with a smile and a nod to do the same with the end of the line. Several turns around a cleat or piling will hold even a good sized boat long enough for a crew member to get to it in order to make the line more secure. If the wind is strong, have the person add another turn or two.

Once you master the simplest line throwing skill, there are two other line throwing skills worthy of learning:

- The ability to throw a bight of the line over a piling, cleat, or other object: This is done very much like throwing a line as mentioned above, only the coils in both hands are let go in an arcing motion, almost simultaneously, while maintaining a grip on each end of the line in separate hands.

- The ability to lasso something, such as a piling or cleat: This toss is more successful if the loop, relative to the item being lassoed, is large and the "front" of the loop is heaved, in an arcing motion, to slightly lead the "back" of the loop. This timing and motion usually causes the loop to open up. This is a most difficult toss, even in the best of circumstances. So if you fail, don't be disappointed as very few folks can achieve a high percent of success, in fact, most people's success rate is very low. If you miss, just laugh it off while re-coiling, then re-throw.

Appendix 4

PARADOX OF STRETCH

The stretch in rope used in anchoring is different from the stretch that occurs in rope used in land-based activities. In land-based activities, stretch usually has only a static component. But, in anchoring, stretch in a rope rode (or snubber) has both a static component, and a repetitive, dynamic component.

With an anchored boat, static stretch is the result of the wind; this stretch changes only when the wind speed changes. This type of stretch does not cause chafe unless: 1) The wind's direction changes, and this usually has to occur repeatedly; or, 2) The rope lies on a sharp edge. If the fibers are stretched too far–the rope having too low of a Design Factor–this, too, can harm the rope.

Dynamic stretch, however, is different. It is caused by seas, waves, and wind gusts, so it comes and goes. It is this repetitive stretching and relaxing of the rope that's responsible for most chafe. It also produces friction between the rope's fibers, and it is this friction that causes heat. This heat can become so severe that the rope's fibers melt. When rope fibers melt, they leave evidence–shiny areas on the rope's surface or little hard nodules within the rope's fibers. Even if the temperature does not reach 450° F, the temperature required for Nylon or polyester fibers to melt, this heat nonetheless results in a loss of strength–e.g., at 300° F, the rope sustains a 30 percent loss of strength.

You probably can't eliminate problems associated with dynamic stretch. Instead, your goal should be to have enough stretch to cushion surge loads, but not so much stretch that the rope suffers chafe and a build-up of heat that could otherwise be avoided.

As odd as it may at first sound, "too much stretch" in the rode or snubber allows for shock loading. Here's why: As the wind blows, it "uses up" some of the rope's stretchability, leaving whatever amount of stretch that remains in the rode (or snubber) to cushion surge loads. In light winds, this is unimportant, since the load on the rope is light enough that plenty of stretch remains available to cushion the relatively light surge loads. But, this is not so as the wind speed rises.

Since the wind load goes up exponentially, while stretch resistance is more linear, as the wind increases in speed, the wind pulls more and more stretch out of the rope, with less and less surge-cushioning stretch left remaining in the rope. Eventually, if the wind becomes strong enough, there is not enough stretch left in the rope to cushion the surge loads. In extreme cases, this is observed as a rode or snubber that is "bar tight". Surge loads that are not fully cushioned turn into shock loads, and even mild shock loads, studies have shown, can double, triple or more, the load on the rope. All this applies to dock lines, too.

Over-stretching, inadequate cushioning, chafe, too much friction, and shock loading would be bad enough if any one of these factors was imposed on the rope, but when two or more occur in concert with one another, the effects are compounded. And as the load on the rope increases beyond 20 percent of its tensile strength, the damage to the rope is accelerated, while the rope's ability to cushion surge loads continues to lessen. This is very likely why during heavy weather you will often see a rope rode, snubber, or dock line that appears to be doing fine, suddenly starts to chafe, and then, very rapidly parts.

PARADOX OF STRETCH

Fortunately, when rope rodes, snubbers, and dock lines are sized so that the maximum loads on them remain no higher than 12.5 percent of the rope's tensile strength—a Design Factor of 8—not only do the ropes have plenty of strength and greater resistance to chafe and melting, they also retain plenty of stretch to cushion surge loads, but, they must also be of long enough length in order to do so (see Chapter 5).

> **LINES THAT CHAFE TOO EASILY**
>
> As mentioned in Chapter 5, the solution is simple: use a bigger, stronger line, and if the line, by itself, cannot be long enough to adequately cushion surge loads, install a device that can provide the necessary cushioning. One such device is a big, black, stretchable band, marketed under the brand name "Dock Line Snubber". No doubt there are other devices which can do the same.

When a boat is anchored where the protection from seas is moderate, the wind and seas each contribute half of the load on the ground tackle. If protection from seas is even better, the wind will have to be higher for the load on the rode to exceed the rode's 12.5 percent point, as there are no seas to contribute to the load. On the other hand, if protection from the seas is poorer, the 12.5 percent point of loading on the rope will develop at a lower wind speed, as the portion of the load contributed by the seas is greater. This is one explanation as to why the same size rope used on similar boats in two different locations, during the same storm can have greatly different amounts of damage.

Appendix 5

KELLETS

A kellet, aka: sentinel or angle, is a weight, hung from or attached to an anchor rode, primarily to increase the rode's catenary. Any weight, from a lead weight, to an extra anchor can be used as a kellet, even a cement-filled bucket. A kellet for a 40-foot boat typically weighs 35-50 lbs., though this is not a firmly fixed figure. For this, as well as other sized boats, the kellet, relative to the boat's size, can be heavier or lighter.

Kellets are typically attached to a saddle, which can be a purpose-made item, a large shackle, or even just a loop of chain or hefty line. Once the saddle is installed around the rode and the kellet attached to it, they are allowed to slide down into position, generally halfway to the anchor. This positioning of the kellet is controlled by an attached line which is lead back to and belayed on the vessel. It is also acceptable, if it is possible to do so, to just position the weight on the rode and tie it in place.

Using heavier anchor chain can substitute for a kellet, and two advantages of this approach are: 1) The additional weight is ever-present; and, 2) There are no other pieces and parts to be deployed, recovered, or stowed. On the other hand, the weight of heavier chain in a rode locker at the bow can affect the boat's trim and handling, unlike a kellet which can be removed and stowed elsewhere.

As mentioned, the "normal" position for a kellet is about halfway from the boat to the anchor, but:

- To further decrease the rode-to-bottom angle, move the kellet closer to the anchor.

- To increase surge cushioning, move the kellet closer to the anchor.

- To reduce a vessel's swing room, its tendency to shear back and forth, or horse around, the kellet is best left lying on the seabed.

- To alleviate the effects of resonance, the best placement of the kellet will most likely require experimentation.

- To know how far down the rode the kellet is positioned, mark the kellet-positioning line at easy-to-remember intervals.

As helpful as a kellet or heavier chain can be, there is a limitation to its effectiveness. As that old timer said—"at 40 knots, there ain't no catenary", and this tends to be true even with the use of heavier chain or that of a kellet.

Once the wind speed rises to the point where the rode's catenary significantly disappears, so does the effectiveness of the kellet or that of heavier chain. And keep in mind that with a rope rode or when the protection from seas is poor, the rode's catenary will disappear at wind speeds of less than 40 knots.

If the wind speed will approach the level where the catenary will disappear, consider these better alternatives to using a kellet:

- Let out more rode; for example, without any contributing catenary, a scope of 10:1 produces that 6 degree rode-to-bottom angle which considerably enhances an anchor's holding ability; deploying more than 10:1 scope may sometimes be necessary to maintain this angle (see Chapter 8).

- To cushion surge loads, use long, Nylon snubbers (see Chapter 5).

- To minimize swing room or the boat's tendency to shear back and forth, employ multiple anchors (see Appendix 7).

Appendix 6

SCOWING, KEDGING, DRUDGING & SPRINGING

SCOWING AN ANCHOR

Scowing an anchor is an ingeniously simple, age-old technique used on an anchor, enabling it to be pulled out backward should it become fouled in the bottom.

To scow an anchor, the rode is first attached at the crown of the anchor–the fluke end–then lead up along the anchor's shank, pulled snug and loosely lashed to the anchor's head with a couple of turns of "small stuff", or those ubiquitous cable ties.

Most any anchor can be scowed as long as the arrangement of the rode does not interfere with the anchor's ability to function as designed.

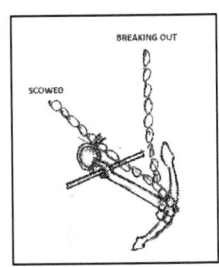

To retrieve a scowed anchor, fouled or otherwise, the boat is brought up over the anchor, the rode hauled taut, and a strain taken on the rode strong enough to break the lashings. As long as the rode also has not fouled, once the lashings have broken, with the rode now able to pull on the "rear" of the anchor, the anchor will usually come out backward.

Since the strain on the rode must break the lashings, the "small stuff" making up the lashings should be as light and as few as feasible, but not so light and few that the pull on the anchor with a low rode-to-bottom angle will cause them to part. Unless you have experience using this technique, it will more than likely be a trial and error process, and until perfected it is best to maintain an anchor watch in case the lashings break before you need them to.

To avoid strain on the "small stuff", as the wind strengthens and the rode starts to straighten, sufficient rode must be deployed, aiming for a rode-to-bottom angle of 6 degrees or less, an angle which, once the rode's catenary has started to straighten, may require a scope of 10:1 or more.

Also, a rise in the wind speed, coupled with a shift in the direction of the wind or current, can result in a lateral strain placed on these lashings, and if sufficient, will result in the lashing parting. In these circumstances, additional anchor(s) should be pre-emptively deployed in a pattern to prevent the lashings from parting (see Appendix 7).

KEDGING

Kedging is the act of deploying an anchor and using its rode to pull the vessel along. Although most any anchor, if it can set in the involved bottom and is small enough or light enough to be taken out by dinghy or by swimming it out, can be used for kedging, high holding power-to-weight anchors, such as Danforth-style anchors, are a good choice. Fortress FX and Guardian series, being aluminum, are even lighter, making them even more convenient for this purpose. One big plus of the Fortress FX series is that the fluke angle of this anchor can be adjusted for use in either sand or mud, enhancing its holding power. For a bottom with weeds, a fisherman-style anchor would be the design of choice.

When kedging, the use of crew muscle, windlass, winch, or tackle are all options that might need to be called into play, while turning blocks may be necessary to provide fair leads.

DRUDGING

Drudging is a technique that allows the boat, by adjusting the length of the rode deployed, to intentionally drag its anchor, providing control over the boat's speed or direction of movement. Though usually done from the bow, drudging can be done from any location on the vessel from which the rode can be belayed. If this location is not conducive to deploying the anchor, the anchor can be deployed elsewhere and the rode brought to and belayed at the desired location. If conditions prevent the safe recovery of the anchor at the time, the rode can be buoyed, then slipped, and the anchor recovered at a later time.

SPRINGING A BOAT AT ANCHOR

Springing a boat at anchor is employed for such things as to allow the boat to lie more comfortably to the seas or current or to orient the boat to take better advantage of wind or sun.

To do so, a line is attached to a point on the rode that is well beyond the bow, then lead, adjusted for length, and belayed amidships or farther aft.

This spring line can be attached to the rode using a knot, such as a rolling hitch, or attached around the rode using a block. Snatch blocks can be opened, placed around the line and then closed, making them more convenient to use than threading a closed block onto the rode which requires doing so from one end of the rode or the other.

Springing a boat is a technique that can also be used with a parachute anchor, to get the boat to lie better to the seas when lying a-hull.

Appendix 7

MULTIPLE ANCHOR ARRANGEMENTS

With one anchor down, a boat is "anchored"; with two or more anchors down, each is on its own rode, the boat is "moored". An "anchor mooring" is one that is expected to be picked up and carried aboard the boat, being different from a "seabed mooring", one that is "permanently" installed. For the grammarians among us, to say "multiple anchor moor", though that term might be used, is every bit as incorrect as saying "knots per hour".

USES OF MULTIPLE ANCHORS

- To limit the boat's swing room or to keep the boat away from dangers;
- To prevent fouling the rode on the boat's anchor or on other objects;
- To minimize side loading an anchor, thus minimizing opportunities for the anchor to trip, drag, bend, or break.
- To orient the boat to wind, seas, or current.

PLEASE TAKE NOTE

As mentioned in Chapter 6, the purpose of using multiple anchors is not to "catch" the boat after the other anchor trips, drags, deforms, or breaks, but, instead, to prevent that anchor from tripping, dragging, deforming, or breaking to begin with. This is another one of those subtle, but important, distinctions in anchoring that should be understood.

"THE BIG 5"

Each anchor in an "anchor moor" is subject to "The Big 5"–each anchor should be of a design that can set on its own in the type of bottom in which it is being used, and be large enough to have the necessary holding power. In addition, adequate scope must be deployed for each anchor, all components must have the requisite strength, and good anti-chafe techniques must be employed.

HAMMERLOCK MOOR

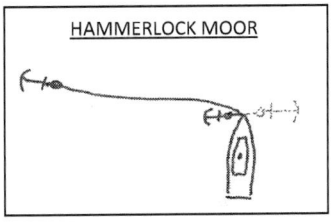

The Hammerlock Moor is simply setting a second anchor off the bow, but close-in and on the shortest scope to which the anchor will tend to remain set or to slowly drag. This technique is one way to reduce a boat's horsing or shearing around, or to limit the boat's swing room.

TWO ANCHORS- "V" PATTERN

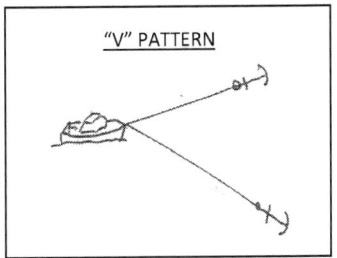

Two anchors are deployed, so that their rodes form a "V" with an angle, usually, of not less than 30°.

BAHAMIAN MOOR

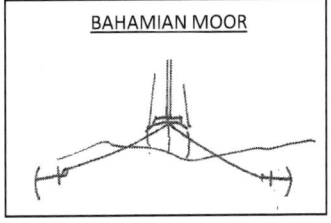

Two anchors are deployed 180° to one another, with both rodes made fast at the bow of the boat.

MULTIPLE ANCHOR ARRANGEMENTS

TWO ANCHORS- BOW AND STERN PATTERN

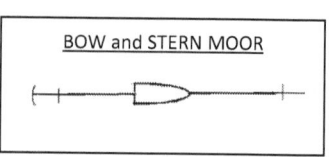

BOW and STERN MOOR

Two anchors are deployed "in-line", 180° to one another. One rode is made fast at the bow, the other rode made fast at the stern. Should the wind come abeam of the boat, the load on the ground tackle will be 50 percent higher than if the boat were able to swing into the wind. The gear will need to be sized for this increased load. (See deployment instructions at the end of this chapter.)

CIRCULAR PATTERN

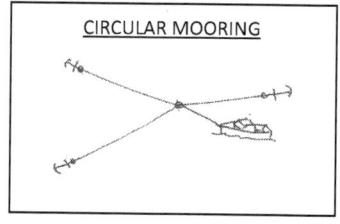

CIRCULAR MOORING

Three anchors, or more, are deployed in a circular pattern with the boat as the center point. Each rode can be lead to and be belayed at the bow of the boat, or to a central point, with a pendant that leads from this central point to the boat.

AVOIDING TWISTS, KINKS AND HOCKLES IN THE RODE

When multiple anchors are set off the bow, an option is to bring the rodes together at one common point, usually a large steel ring, with a single, hefty pendant lead from the ring to the boat, possibly with a swivel placed in-line. This ring must be large enough to accommodate all of the rodes, plus the pendant.

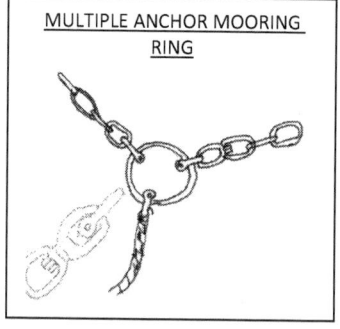

MULTIPLE ANCHOR MOORING RING

This ring can be an off-the-shelf product, but it should have a tensile strength four times that of the maximum load that will be on the ground tackle. You can also have a ring like this made locally by a welder or machine shop using the largest diameter steel rod that will fit through the opening in the shackles you plan to use.

This ring will also need to have an inside diameter large enough to comfortably accept all of the lines or their shackles. This takes a larger ring than what many folks, at first, think will be big enough. As an example, a ring that will comfortably accommodate four ½ inch galvanized shackles can be made out of ¾ inch rod, but will require an inside diameter of over five inches if the shackles are to fit without jamming against one another. Should more than four shackles be used, the inside diameter of the ring will need to increase substantially.

EXPERIMENTING WITH YOUR ANCHORS

Earlier in this chapter we mentioned that the purpose of setting a second anchor is not to catch the boat if it drags, but, instead, to prevent the anchor from dragging, or maybe from bending. But a second anchor can also be used to safely test another anchor. If the second anchor is "big-enough", given sufficient rode, and can set in the bottom on its own, it can be laid out with the intention to "catch" the boat in case the "test" anchor trips, drags, or the boat breaks free.

We've often used our 70 lb. Luke anchor in a variety of conditions to experiment like this. We make fast the bitter end of the rode, drop the anchor, and arrange sufficient rode, belayed, but left slack, or flaked-down on deck ready to run out should the "test" anchor drag.

DEPLOYING "BOW and STERN" ANCHORS

With sufficient rode on each anchor and bitter ends made fast, position the boat, then lower and set the first anchor. As the rode is let out, reposition the boat at a distance from the first anchor of at least twice the length of the longest intended scope. When in position, drop the second anchor. Then, letting out the second rode, reposition the boat back between the two anchors, taking in the slack that develops in the first rode. Set the second anchor, belay the rodes, and if needed, install snubbers. Anchors are retrieved by reversing the sequence.

There are times when circumstances dictate which anchor–bow or stern–goes first. If either rode has to be handed, chain, being onerous to hand is better reserved for use only when and where chafe is a concern, otherwise an all-rope rode is friendliest on the hands. Wind or current, maybe muscle, can often be substituted for engine power when positioning the boat. If the "big boat's" engine power cannot overcome the wind or current, you might have to resort to the use of a dinghy or swimming to get the second anchor out. This basic procedure can be adapted to set anchors in other patterns.

CAUTION PERTAINING TO THE USE OF MULTIPLE ANCHORS

With multiple anchors, while the use of undersized anchors may be successful during mild or short-duration conditions, during severe or prolonged conditions, things are different. As the boat veers back and forth, the load also alternates back and forth, cycling from one anchor, to the other. Then, since no one undersized anchor can hold the boat on its own, this alternating loading causes each anchor to drag, usually little by little. If the conditions persist long enough, the anchors will eventually migrate toward, then foul one another. Once fouled, neither of the anchors will be able to function as designed, with the result being that they will either trip, or continue to drag, usually faster. Instead, be certain that each anchor in an anchor moor is large enough to be able to hold the boat on its own in the type of bottom in which they are used.

Appendix 8

ETIQUETTE IN TIGHT QUARTERS

The use of "too much scope" is often questioned by some crews, particularly when room to anchor is in short supply. But it is Mother Nature who dictates the amount of scope that is necessary, not some crew's arbitrarily imposed desires. Fortunately, the manner in which situations like this should be dealt with has long been established, both legally and practically–the first boat to anchor may do so in any manner that its crew deems necessary, any boat that follows has the legal obligation to:

- Avoid fouling any previously anchored boat's swing radius;
- To position their boat so to not interfere with any previously anchored boat's ability to get underway;
- Take into account both present and future wind, current, and weather; and,
- Allow room for previously anchored boats, at their discretion, to pay out more rode or place additional anchors.

Should the latter arriving boat violate any of these mandates, the first boat at anchor is legally obligated, conditions permitting, to warn the latter of the violation. If this warning is needed, it should be done in a clear, but hopefully, tactful manner. Whether the latter arriving boat needs to move or not depends on the circumstances, but regardless of any decision, they remain responsible for the consequences. (U.S. Admiralty Court, Decision No. 124-5861, 1956.)

From a legal perspective, if giving notice like this is necessary, any

ETIQUETTE IN TIGHT QUARTERS

action taken and response, should be noted in the vessel's log book. If the offending vessel could not be warned, an explanation as to why it was not done should also be noted in the log.

These guidelines also applies to those whose anchor comes out of the bottom, whether intentional or due to some mishap, such as dragging, tripping, or breaking free. Once this occurs, that boat has lost any "preferred" status and is transformed into a "later arrival". Now being a "later arrival", it must adhere to the applicable rules as if it had just arrived. This boat does not have the right to its previous spot unless the other anchored boats extend it that courtesy.

The final word on this, what often turns into a contentious situation, is simple: if there is not enough room for a later arrival to anchor securely and safely without interfering with another anchored boat, then that later arriving boat is under an obligation to go elsewhere, even if doing so affords less protection or requires more or heftier gear.

Those who do not prepare for all these contingencies have no right to impose the consequences of their poor planning on others and are solely responsible for the outcome. On the other hand, if you are the offended vessel, when all is said and done, sometimes it's just less stressful, easier, and probably even safer to avail yourself of the option to just up anchor yourself and go elsewhere.

Appendix 9

OTHER SUGGESTED READINGS

HIGHLY RECOMMENDED

The Complete Book of Anchoring and Mooring- Earl Hinz

Chapman- Piloting, Seamanship and Small Boat Handling- Jonathan Eaton

OTHER BOOKS

The Annapolis Book of Seamanship- John Rousmaniere

The Complete Anchoring Handbook- Alain Poiraud, Achim Ginsberg-Klemmt, and Erika Ginsberg-Klemmt

Happy Hooking- The Art of Anchoring- Blackwell and Blackwell

Anchoring and Mooring the Cruising Multihull- Mark Johnson

Complete Guide to Anchors and Anchoring- David Lynn

Anchoring and Mooring Techniques- Alain Gree

GLOSSARY

ABYC: American Boat and Yacht Council: A private organization in the U.S.A. that promulgates standards for building boats and the installation of the various systems within a boat.

Abeam: Lying at right angles to the vessel's fore-and-aft centerline.

Alloy: A substance that is a mixture of two or more metals.

Anchor Ball: A shape in the form of a black ball displayed in the forward part of the vessel from sunrise until sundown to indicate that the vessel is at anchor.

Anchored: When a boat "rides" or "lies" to a single anchor rode, though it is possible to have two anchors in tandem on one rode. (See "Moored")

Athwartship: Lying along the ship's width, at right angles to the vessel's fore-and-aft centerline.

Backing: In the northern hemisphere, a counterclockwise change or shifting of the wind around the compass points, from east to north, for example. (See "Veer")

Bank: A large area of shallow water, as in the Bahama Banks.

Belay: To make a line secure to a pin, cleat, bitt or other like item; or, a command to stop or halt action.

Bend: A knot used to connect a line to another object.

Bending Load: A force applied to an item in a direction other than along the item's center line; aka: side load.

Bight: Any central part of a rope, distinct from the ends and the standing part; a curve or arc in a rope, no more than a semicircle; an indentation in the coastline lying between two promontories, but larger than a bay.

Bill: The point or front edge of an anchor's fluke or palm.

Bitt: A vertical post extending above the deck of a vessel for attaching lines, usually for the purpose of mooring.

BL: Breaking Load

Bobstay: A stay from the stem of a boat to the end of a bowsprit used to counteract the upward pull of the forestay.

Bollard: A large, solid post on a wharf, pier or quay for securing mooring lines; can also be fixed to the deck of a ship.

Bower: A term for the anchor that is kept on the bow of a vessel; aka: bow anchor.

Brait: A specific form of braiding fibers into cordage; aka: plait.

Break Load (BL): The point at which an item, with a consistently increasing force, will break; can be noted as Minimum Breaking Load (MBL), Average Breaking Load (ABL), or Ultimate Breaking Load (UBL).

Breaking Free: When a vessel unintentionally becomes free from its anchor or mooring.

Bridle: A line or wire secured at both ends in order to distribute a strain between two points; a short length of rope or wire with a line attached at the mid-point.

Capstan: A vertical spool-shaped rotating drum around which cable, hawser or chain is wound for hoisting anchors, sails and other heavy weights.

Catenary: The sag in a rope, cable or chain due to its own weight.

Chafe: Abrasion, wear or damage to a line caused by rubbing against another object.

Chain Locker: A compartment in which chain is stowed.

Chain Pipe: A pipe, generally of large relative diameter, through which chain passes into the chain locker.

Chain Stopper: A mechanical device installed along the path of a rode, used to stop off a chain rode. It is also a plug, used to prevent water from entering.

Chain Wheel: A special type of drum or sprocket on a windlass constructed to handle chain; aka: wildcat or gypsy.

Chandlery: A marine hardware store.

Classification Societies: Worldwide reputable and experienced societies which undertake inspections of and provide advice on the hull and machinery of a ship; or, private organizations who supervise vessels during and after construction in respect to vessel seaworthiness, and who rate vessels into grades or "classes" according to the society's rules for each particular type of vessel.

Cleat: A fitting of wood or metal, secured to the vessel, with two horns around which ropes are made fast.

Cleat Hitch: A specific manner in belaying a line to a cleat. When the bitter end forms a bight in the line and this bight is brought under the last riding turn, the hitch is termed "slipped".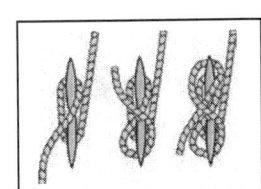

Clocked: Movement in a circular pattern.

Clocking Winds: Wind direction that circles around the compass points in a clockwise direction.

Combination Rode: A rode that is part rope and part chain.

Cordage Institute: The organization in the U.S.A. responsible for establishing, for its members, the standards to which rope is manufactured.

De Rigueur: Routine

Deck Pipe: A pipe, generally of large diameter, through which rope passes into the rope locker.

Design Factor: The ratio of the difference between an item's Working Load Limit and its Breaking Point.

Dock: Formally, a dock is the water area where a vessel lies when it is made fast to a shore installation; informally, a structure bordering the water area to which vessels are made fast.

Dock Line: A line used to secure a vessel in a slip or alongside a pier or quay. (Not to be confused with docking line; see below)

Docked: Formally, when a vessel is in dry dock; informally, when a vessel is secured to a dock.

Docking: Informally, the process of going from underway to being made fast alongside a dock or pier.

Docking Line: A line used when bringing a vessel into a slip or alongside a pier or quay, thrown to a person, over a cleat or around a piling. (Not to be confused with dock line, which secures the vessel in a slip or alongside a pier or quay. See above.)

Double-dipped: A term used in galvanizing when the item remains in the zinc for a longer than normal period of time, allowing a thicker layer of zinc to be deposited.

Drag: The resistance to movement; or, when an anchor cannot hold its position.

Drift: The speed of a current.

Drudging: Controlling the speed and direction of movement of a vessel by dragging an anchor in a controlled manner, accomplished by controlling the length of an anchor's rode, which determines the anchor's ability to drag.

Extrapolate: To estimate something unknown on the basis of known facts.

Fetch: The distance that the wind or sea has to travel over water, unimpeded by land or other objects.

Fetch-up: To stop suddenly.

Fisherman Anchor: A traditionally shaped anchor having flukes perpendicular to the stock of the anchor and connected by a shank.

Fluke-to-shank Angle: The angle formed by the shank of an anchor and its flukes.

Foul: Tangle, entangle or obstruct.

Foul Bottom: A bottom likely to obstruct, tangle or entangle an anchor.

Freeboard: The distance between a vessel's waterline and its main deck. (Freeboard can be different at different points along a vessel's deck and varies with the load of fuel, water, cargo and stores onboard).

Freshening the Nip: Easing off a line a short distance so that a different part of the line will be subject to chafe from the surface touching the line.

Gale Force: Winds of 34 – 47 knots.

Galling: Cold welding of one metal to another.

Ground Tackle: A collective term for the anchor, anchor rode, and all of the associated gear necessary for its use.

Gypsy: A special type of drum or sprocket on a windlass constructed to handle chain; aka: wildcat or chain wheel.

Hallmark: An identifying mark.

Hammerlock Moor: When a vessel is at anchor and an additional anchor is deployed on the shortest scope possible that will allow this additional anchor to remain set; used to minimize a vessel's movement.

Hand: The degree of tightness, during manufacture, in which strands of a rope are twisted together, aka: lay; the manipulation of an item by hand.

Haul: To pull.

Hawse: That part of a vessel's bow where the hawse holes and hawse pipes are situated.

Hawse Hole: A hole in the hull for mooring lines, cables or chain to run through.

Hawse Pipe: A large pipe that connects a hawse hole with the deck through which an anchor rode is drawn, usually by a windlass.

Heave: A linear movement up and down in line with the vessel's vertical axis.

Heaving Line: A small diameter line, often with its end weighted, thrown to a line handler. The heaving line is fastened to a larger line so the larger, heavier line can be pulled to the line handler.

Helix Mooring: A long pole, with a helix-like device along a portion of its length, which is driven into the seabed bottom and is used to moor a vessel.

Helmsman: The person who steers the vessel.

Hitch: A knot used to secure a line to another object or to another line.

Holding Power: The amount of force that an anchor can resist.

Horsing: Lateral movement, back and forth, of the bow of a vessel at anchor; aka: sailing at anchor.

Housed: When an object is settled in a fitting that is designed to hold it.

Idiosyncrasy: A peculiarity or mannerism.

ISO: International Standards Organization.

Kedging: To move a vessel by setting out an anchor and pulling the vessel toward the anchor by hauling on the rode.

Kellet: A weight added to a rode to increase the rode's catenary; aka: sentinel.

Knot: A method of attaching cordage to itself, to other cordage or to a fitting; a measure of speed, equaling one nautical mile per hour.

Lay: The degree of tightness to which strands are twisted together during manufacture; aka: hand.

Lead: A section of rode leading from the anchor; the direction in which a line goes.

Line: Rope or cordage that has been put into use aboard or employed on a vessel.

Main Bower: A vessel's primary, everyday bow anchor.

Make Fast: To attach a line to something so that it will not release.

Messenger Line: A detachable line hitched to a larger, heavier line, used to pull the larger line towards a goal, or a detachable line which is hitched to a vessel's rode, typically used in conjunction with some form of mechanical advantage, to recover the ground tackle.

Midshipman's Hitch- *see* Rolling Hitch

Mixed Rode: A rode comprised of part rope and part cable or chain.

Monkey Fist: A large, specifically formed knot in the end of a line to aid in throwing.

Moored: When a boat lies to two or more anchors, each on a separate rode, or is attached to a permanent structure. (Not to be confused with tandem anchors, which are two anchors attached to a single rode.)

Mouse: Wrappings of small yarn, twine or other material to hold a pin or other item in place.

Mousing Wire: Used to mouse; aka safety wire.

NACM: National Association of Chain Manufacturers.

Negligence: Failure to exercise the degree of care that, under the circumstances, the law requires. Failure to do the required thing; being careless or inattentive.

Oscillation: Any of, or a combination of the various movements that a boat can undergo while in the water–roll, pitch, yaw, surge, sway, and heave.

Palm: That portion of a fisherman-style anchor which corresponds to a fluke on other anchors.

Paradox: A statement that seems contradictory.

Peened: Hammered over, as is done to a rivet to fix it in place.

Pendant: A short line used for a specific purpose; a line by which a boat is connected to a mooring buoy or other object; a short rope hanging from a spar having at its free end a spliced-in thimble or block; aka: pennant.

Pennant: see pendant.

Percent of Stretch: The amount of stretch, by percentage, in cordage under load.

Pitch: A vessel's motion, rotating around its transverse axis, causing the fore and aft ends to rise and fall.

PL: Proof Load

Plait: A specific form of braiding fibers into cordage; aka: brait.

Proof Load: The point at which an item, with a consistently increasing force, will deform.

Reef: Reducing the amount of area.

Rock Bottom: A bottom composed of solid rock or coral.

Rocky Bottom: A bottom made up of many broken pieces of rock.

Rode: A line, cable or chain that connects a vessel to its anchor.

Rode Locker: A compartment in which rode is stowed.

Rode Marker: Marks placed on a rode indicating the distance from the rode's outboard end.

Rode-to-bottom Angle: The angle formed by the rode/shank combination relative to the anchor's flukes.

Roll: A vessel's rotational side-to-side motion about its fore-and-aft (longitudinal) axis

Rolling Hitch: A knot made by passing the bitter end of a line around its standing part, or an object, twice, then carrying it back across these two turns, around the standing part and through the bight formed where the bitter end crossed across the initial two turns. (Rolling Hitch/Midshipman's Hitch/Tautline Hitch are the same knot, differing only by the item around which the knot is made.)

Rope: A thick cord made of inter-twisted strands of fibers.

Rope Locker: A compartment in which rope is stowed.

Rope Pipe: A pipe, usually of large relative diameter, through which rope passes into the rope locker.

Resonance: When a vessel's motion and the period of the waves surrounding it closely correspond, often exacerbating the motion of the vessel.

Round Turn: A loop in a line which crosses itself; a closed loop.

Safety Factor (SF): The difference between an item's Working Load Limit and its Proof Load.

Safety Wire: See mousing wire.

Samson Post: A large vertical post fixed to a vessel around which lines are belayed.

Scope: The length of rode in use relative to the depth of water plus freeboard at the bow as measured from the deck.

Scowing: The fastening of a rode to an anchor's crown, running the rode taught along the shank and making it fast to the anchor's head with a few turns of light seizing or "small stuff". By pulling on the anchor's rode, this small stuff can be broken which allows the anchor to be pulled out backward.

Seiche: A standing wave or short period oscillation in the level of an enclosed, or partly enclosed body of water, not due to tidal forces.

Sentinel: A weight placed on the rode to increase the rode's catenary; aka: kellet.

Set: A secure grip on the bottom by an anchor; the direction of current; or, the angle of sails to the wind.

Shakedown Cruise: A trip undertaken to discover and resolve problems with a vessel.

Shock Load: A load that results from rapid application of a force.

Side Load: Any load on an item in a direction other than along its axis; aka: bending load.

Slipped: A term used when the working end of a line is doubled back and lead under a turn, so that by pulling on the end of the line, this loop is withdrawn; or, is let go.

Slipped Knot: When a knot is finished being tied by forming a loop with the end of the line and this loop is slid under one of the knot's turns, allowing, with a pull on the end of the knot a release of the knot's security. The knot that is typically used to tie shoe laces is a good example of a double slipped knot. A slipped knot is not to be confused with a Slip Knot, a specific form of a knot, as is illustrated by Figure 529, in *The Ashely Book of Knots*.

Sloop: A single mast sailing vessel with fore- and aft-rigged sails, a mainsail and a jib.

Small Stuff: Cordage of a very small diameter, less than ¼" in diameter.

Snub: To stop the running out of a line by taking at least one turn around an object such as a cleat or bollard; or, to suddenly stop.

Snubber: A line attached to an anchor rode, and made fast to a strong point on the vessel. Used to remove the load off the mechanism of a windlass, to cushion surge loads, or to save the rode from chafe.

Snubber Braid: A braided section on the end of a snubber, put in to allow the snubber have a better grip.

Spring lines: lines that lead forward or aft on a vessel used to keep the vessel from moving ahead or astern.

Springing the boat: The technique of using lines lead forward or aft from a vessel to a fixed object, such as a cleat, or piling, or anchor rode, to change the orientation or position of the vessel.

Squall: A brief, violent windstorm, with an increase of wind speed of 16 knots or more and lasting more than 1 minute.

Standing Part: That part of a rope which is inactive, as opposed to the bight and working end.

Stay: A line, chain or wire lead forward or aft along the centerline of the vessel for support of the mast.

Stop-off: Secured in place, usually with some form of cable, either fiber or wire, or with chain, often employing a suitable connector.

Storm Force: 48 – 63 knots of wind.

Stretch Length: The length to which a line will extend when placed under a specific percentage of loading.

Strong Point: An object to which a line may be made fast and is strong enough to resist the force applied to it.

Surge: The action of seas or waves against a vessel; to ease out on a line, keeping its speed under control; a linear movement forward and backward in line with the vessel's longitudinal axis.

Surge Loads: The forces put on a vessel and its ground tackle due to the seas

.

Sway: Linear movement athwartship in line with the vessel's transverse axis.

Tail: The end of a line; hold or pull on a line.

Tandem: Two or more items aligned one behind the other. The term tandem anchors denotes two anchors attached in series to a single rode.

Tautline Hitch- *see* Rolling Hitch

Tensile Strength: The amount of strength an item has in straight-line pull before breaking.

Tether: A line attached between an object and the boat.

Throat: The location where two lines meet at an angle; the forward, upper corner of a four-sided sail.

Trip: When an anchor's flukes break out of the bottom.

Trip Line: A line attached to the crown of an anchor, used to pull the anchor free should it become fouled.

Turn: A loop in a line which does not cross itself; an open loop.

Up and Down: The position of an anchor's rode when the vessel is over the anchor and the rode has been hauled taut.

Veer: To let out, or, in the northern hemisphere, a shifting of the wind around the compass points in a clockwise direction. The opposite of "backing".

Warping Drum: A special type of drum on a windlass constructed to handle rope.

Way: The movement of a vessel through the water. A vessel moving through the water is said to be underway or to have way on.

Weighing Anchor: Raising an anchor in preparation for getting underway.

Wildcat: A special type of drum or sprocket on a windlass constructed to handle chain; aka: chain gypsy or chain wheel.

Winch: A metal drum-shaped device used to provide leverage or increase hauling power when hoisting or trimming sails, to load or discharge cargo, or for hauling in lines.

Wind Speed: Officially, the speed of the wind as measured at a height of 30 feet above the water in an area specifically designed to not have any obstructions to the wind.

Windage: The area on a vessel giving resistance to wind.

Windlass: A special form of winch used to hoist anchors, in which the drum(s) are arranged horizontally.

WLL: Working Load Limit.

Working Load Limit: The maximum load for which an item is rated; aka: Work Load Limit (WL), Safe Working Limit (SWL), Rated Capacity (RC), or Rated Value (RV).

Yaw: An angular movement, swinging the vessel's bow or stern side to side about the vessel's vertical axis.

INDEX